ENGLISH-CANADIAN
THEATRE

Perspectives on Canadian Culture

JUDITH SALTMAN
Modern Canadian Children's Books

EUGENE BENSON & L.W. CONOLLY
English-Canadian Theatre

DAVID CLANDFIELD
Canadian Film

Forthcoming:

MICHELLE GADPAILLE
The Canadian Short Story

EDITH FOWKE
Canadian Folklore

PENNY PETRONE
Canadian Indian Literature

MERVIN BUTOVSKY
Canadian Jewish Writers

DAVID KETTERER
Canadian Science Fiction and Fantasy

ALICE VAN WART
Canadian Diaries and Journals

DONNA BENNETT
Canadian Literary Criticism

ENGLISH-CANADIAN THEATRE

Eugene Benson
&
L.W. Conolly

Toronto OXFORD UNIVERSITY PRESS 1987

For
JAMES and REBECCA
and
ORMONDE and SHAUN

Canadian Cataloguing in Publication Data

Benson, Eugene, 1928–
English-Canadian theatre

(Perspectives on Canadian culture)
Bibliography: p.
Includes index.
ISBN 0-19-540583-8

1. Theater—Canada—History 2. Canadian drama
(English)—History and criticism.* I. Conolly,
L. W. (Leonard W.). II. Title. III. Series.

PN2301.B46 1987   792'.0971   C87-094929-2

CONTENTS

Preface   vii

1. Colonialism and Theatre in Canada   1

    THE NATIVE PEOPLES   1

    THE ATLANTIC PROVINCES   2

    ONTARIO AND QUEBEC   8

    NINETEENTH-CENTURY DRAMA   11

    AUDIENCES   21

    EARLY THEATRE IN WESTERN CANADA   23

    FOREIGN COMPANIES AND STARS   31

    CANADIAN COMPANIES AND STARS   36

2. Towards a Canadian Theatrical Identity   43

    THE LITTLE THEATRE MOVEMENT   43

    THE DOMINION DRAMA FESTIVAL   51

    THE WORKERS' THEATRE   57

    RADIO DRAMA   59

    DRAMA AND THE UNIVERSITIES   63

3. Canadian Professional Theatre   68

    GOVERNMENT AND THEATRE   68

    THE LESSONS OF 1967: HERBERT, REANEY, RYGA   73

    THE ALTERNATE THEATRE   85

    THREE ALTERNATE PLAYWRIGHTS: FREEMAN, WALKER, FRENCH   89

    REGIONALISM   95

    NEW BEARINGS   103

    Selected Bibliography   116

    Index   121

Opening of the Academy of Music, Saint John, N.B., 1873.
E.J. Russell. Courtesy The New Brunswick Museum.

PREFACE

English-Canadian Theatre chronicles the rich anglophone theatrical history of Canada. Although much has been written—especially in the last fifteen years—about Canadian drama and theatre, this is the first single study to draw the various discoveries and insights of that scholarship into a single comprehensive survey. Furthermore, critics and historians have tended to focus on Canadian drama or Canadian theatre but not on both. Because we believe firmly that drama and theatre should not be studied in isolation from each other, we have attempted in *English-Canadian Theatre* to combine dramatic criticism and theatre history in such a way as to provide the reader with an evaluation of Canadian dramatic literature in English as it emerged— slowly and tenuously—within the context of performance. Although references to francophone theatrical activity are both inevitable and desirable in any history of anglophone drama and theatre in Canada, extensive discussion of the wealth of tradition and achievement in Canadian francophone theatre lies beyond the scope of this study.

While writing this book, we were also editing a much longer volume—the forthcoming *Oxford Companion to Canadian Theatre*— which allowed us to benefit from the research undertaken for that work by scholars, theatre critics, directors, designers, and play-wrights across Canada. We gratefully acknowledge our debt to them and to colleagues in the Association for Canadian Theatre History/ l'Association d'histoire du théâtre au Canada, an organization that has taken commendable initiatives in promoting Canadian theatre scholarship. Dr Stephen Johnson, Research Associate for *The Oxford Companion to Canadian Theatre*, has been of great help, especially in finding suitable illustrations, and Herbert Whittaker kindly allowed us access to his collection of theatrical photographs. Jennifer Sumner has also generously assisted in this matter and in typing the text.

Janice Walker, Mary Deverell, Ruth Mickus, Gail McGinnis, and Frances Duiker have provided skilled secretarial and word processing help. We thank Guy Thomas, General Manager of the Stratford Shakespearean Festival, and Lise Rochon, Communications Service, The Canada Council, for providing us with helpful statistics. Heather McCallum, Head, Theatre Section, Metropolitan Toronto Library, has kindly allowed us ready access to the Library's extensive theatrical holdings, and Bruce Barton has been an effective research assistant. Eugene Benson expresses his thanks to the University of Guelph for a 1985–6 Forster Fellowship that allowed him some remission of teaching duties to work on this book and on *The Oxford Companion to Canadian Theatre*. We thank Dr John Black, Chief Librarian of the McLaughlin Library, University of Guelph, and his staff for their help. Patricia Sillers made valuable editorial suggestions and we acknowledge with gratitude the contribution of William Toye, who commissioned us to write this book and provided expert and sympathetic editorial guidance.

1

COLONIALISM AND THEATRE IN CANADA

THE NATIVE PEOPLES

Before the discovery and colonization of North America by Europeans, an indigenous drama of great richness and complexity flourished among the continent's native peoples. In Canada dramas were performed by the Inuit and by many Indian cultures—the Ojibwa, the Iroquois, the Plains' Indians, the Nootka, the Kwakiutl, and others. The Inuit, for example, had special igloos with designated playing and audience areas for their ritual dramas. Their shamans, or mystics, were gifted actors who used masks, stage props, and voice projection (including ventriloquism) to perform with great skill spirit-plays and spirit-dances celebrating initiation, purification, death, and resurrection. Ritualistic performances were designed to benefit the community—by influencing the weather, or curing illnesses, for example—and the community assisted the shaman by participating in song, chant, and dialogue.

The best known of the Indian ritual dramas, the Mystery Play of the British Columbia Kwakiutl Indians, was a vast cycle (like the European medieval Mystery cycles) that encompassed smaller units or spirit-plays and was performed throughout the winter season over a period of four to five months. The most striking ritual drama within the cycle was the Hamatsa or Cannibal performance, which dramatized the story of a novice-hero who leaves his society to do battle with Raven, Hohhuq, and Crooked Beak, the Cannibal Spirit's three bird spirits, and eventually with the Cannibal itself. On his return to society the novice-hero is a daemonic figure who must be tamed through a series of theatrical events that includes dance, song, and speech, resulting in a ritualistic catharsis affecting both actors and audience. The Hamatsa drama, 'one of the most spectacular ceremonials in the world', has been likened by James Hoffman to a five-act play in which the 'whole thrust of the action was the humanizing of a man: he was improved and elevated by means of a pre-planned script that in its structure and in its essential conception as reenactment for a human audience qualifies it as drama.' Commentators on the Kwakiutl Mystery Play point admiringly to its complexity, its theatricality—a combination of speech, song, dance, and mask-play—and to an astonishing prodigality of costumes, stage props, and effects. The beauty and power of the Hamatsa ceremonial play contradict what the critic David Mayer terms 'one of the more cherished concepts of the post-Darwinian historian'—'that drama, along with the other arts, is continually evolving . . . that it grows, improves, progressing from the rudimentary and naive to the fully mature, articulated, and sophisticated drama.' Despite its beauty and power, the drama of the native peoples, however, had little influence on subsequent theatrical developments in Canada, which originated in Europe.

THE ATLANTIC PROVINCES

It is not known precisely when European theatre was first introduced to Canada. As early as Sir Humphrey Gilbert's 1583 expedition to Newfoundland, 'theatrical' activities took place on board ship and in St John's. Edward Hayes, narrator of the voyage, relates that 'we were provided of Musike in good variety: not omitting the least toyes, as Morris dancers, Hobby horsse and Maylike conceits to delight the Savage people, whom we intended to winne by all faire means possible.' The French were also intent on delighting (and colonizing) the 'Savage people', as may be seen in Marc Lescarbot's masque, *Le Théâtre de Neptune en la Nouvelle-France*, performed at the mouth of the Annapolis River on 14 November 1606 to celebrate the return of Jean de Biencourt de Poutrincourt (and Samuel Champlain) to Port Royal (now Annapolis Royal, Nova Scotia) from their explorations along the New England coast. The first play composed and performed in North America, *Le Théâtre de Neptune* (published in Paris in 1609) is a verse drama that was embellished in its first performance by cannons, trumpets, and costumes, and whose cast included some seventy or eighty Frenchmen and Micmac Indians. Lescarbot called his masque a 'réjouissance publique' and it is clearly a celebration of French Imperial power in the New World. French civil and military personnel, together with the powerful Jesuit order, continued to develop the European theatrical tradition in New France, presenting *réceptions* of the *Théâtre de Neptune* variety to honour local or visiting dignitaries, morality plays, and allegories for the edification and indoctrination of students and native peoples, and plays by leading French authors such as Corneille and Racine. Theatrical activity in New France was, however, brought virtually to a halt by the famous 1694 row between Bishop Saint-Vallier and Governor Frontenac over a proposed production of Molière's allegedly blasphemous *Tartuffe*. The Bishop suppressed the play, and theatrical entertainment was enjoyed again in Canada only intermittently until after the 1763 Conquest.

Because eastern Canada was the battleground for English and French hegemony in the seventeenth and eighteenth centuries, and because of fears of American annexation in the nineteenth century, a British military presence—represented by both the army and the navy—was strong. As a means of relieving the tedium of garrison life, and also to foster harmonious relationships with the local communities, the military indulged in a good deal of theatrical activity. William Dyott, an officer garrisoned in Halifax from June 1787 to December 1792, kept a diary that provides valuable insight into some of Nova Scotia's earliest theatre history. We learn that Sheridan's *The School for Scandal* was performed by the officers of the garrison and fleet on 16 December 1788, the female parts being played by two young Halifax boys. On 26 February of the following year the garrison opened a theatre—the New Grand Theatre—with boxes and two pits, offering *The Merchant of Venice* as the first production. Some sixty years later Halifax's garrison was also responsible for refurbishing a large hay barn at the Spring Gardens that became the Theatre Royal. It opened on 2 December 1846 with two contemporary English comedies, J. M. Morton's *The Sentinel* and T. H. Bayly's *You Can't Marry Your Grandmother*. The theatre was gas lit, had boxes seating over 160 people, and numbered seats. In Saint John, where the first recorded theatrical performance took place in 1789, citizens and garrison combined to build the Drury Lane Theatre, which opened on 3 February 1809 with Joseph Holman's *Abroad and at Home* and Isaac Jackman's

All the World's a Stage. The army's assistance in Saint John was matched by the navy's assistance in St John's, where Captain Sir William Eliot, who was stationed there in 1818 and 1819, relates that the navy built a theatre 'the expenses of which, including decorations, scenery, stoves, property, puffing, wigs, wardrobe, light, scene-shifters, theatrical-tailors, and midshipmen's milliners, were entirely defrayed out of the profits of the first month's performance.'

By the middle of the nineteenth century British army and navy personnel had made a substantial contribution to theatre in the Atlantic provinces, not only building theatres but equipping and staffing them. They had also encouraged and welcomed participation from local amateurs. Their resources did not stretch to the construction of theatres as impressive as London's Covent Garden or Drury Lane, but those great theatres provided the models for the more modest houses built in Halifax and other cities. Inevitably the kind of theatre favoured in garrison theatricals derived primarily from the theatre of London, which was familiar to the officers. Ideas about theatrical presentation were imported from England and modified for Canada according to the limited financial and human resources available.

The plays too were also normally imported, but there were some interesting exceptions. Occasionally a military author wrote a play with a Canadian subject and setting, two early examples being dull verse dramas by George Cockings (*The Conquest of Canada*, 1766) and Robert Rogers (*Ponteach*, 1766), neither of which was performed in Canada. By and large, texts of these early plays from the Maritimes have not survived, but advertisements and reviews in newspapers give valuable information. The *Nova Scotia Gazette and Weekly Chronicle*, for example, carried an advertisement on 1 February 1774 for what may have been the first English-Canadian play. *Acadius; or, Love in a Calm* was a three-act comedy concerning (so far as one can tell from the cast-list) a love affair between a naval officer and a merchant's daughter, with comic relief provided by Guttle and Guzzle, two Londoners recently arrived in Nova Scotia. *Acadius*, we learn from a note appended to the advertisement, was a controversial play, alleged to reflect unfavourably on certain local residents.

Elements of personal and political satire figured prominently in eighteenth- and nineteenth-century drama of the Atlantic provinces.

The Triumph of Intrigue by 'O.P.', for example, published serially in the *New Brunswick Courier* of 23 February and 2 and 9 March 1833, attacks the way members of the Legislative Council manipulate the new Lieutenant Governor (Sir Archibald Campbell) for their own private interests. Another political satire (unfortunately not extant), *The Provincial Association; or, Taxing One Another*, caused a riot when it was acted in Saint John in April 1845. Written by Thomas Hill, editor of the *Fredericton Loyalist*, it seems to have been directed against members of a Saint John economic pressure-group known as the Provincial Association. When the play was performed in Saint John at Hopley's Theatre by a company headed by an American actor named Henry Preston, it provoked considerable controversy, culminating in a serious disturbance on the second night. A far-from-unbiased editorial in the *Saint John Morning News* (4 April 1845) attacked the play for bringing into contempt the respectability and 'moral rectitude' of gentlemen of the Saint John community, and, worse, 'the *virtue* of certain ladies' in the city. *Political Intrigue; or, the Best Way to Tar One Another* is another anonymous farce, though it was never performed. An attack on political patronage, it was published in the *Saint John Morning News* of 20 October 1845. Better known is *Measure by Measure; or, the Coalition in Secret Session*, a biting and well-written farce (again anonymous) in pseudo-Shakespearean mock-heroic blank verse, satirizing the political manoeuverings of the New Brunswick Legislature in 1871 when faced with a bill to fund non-sectarian schools. *Measure by Measure*, which was published in seven parts in the *New Dominion and True Humorist*, 25 February to 8 April 1871, was one of several political plays to appear in the *New Dominion* between 1864 and 1871.

The row over *The Provincial Association* and the use of theatre as a political forum in the Maritimes show the existence of an audience that took its drama seriously, especially when the plays were of local origin and involved local issues. With playwrights like Thomas Hill, audiences like those in Saint John, theatres like Saint John's Drury Lane and Halifax's Theatre Royal, and a body of amateur actors in Maritime cities, the conditions for an indigenous Canadian theatrical culture were present. From the beginning, however, there was strong moral opposition to this natural and desirable development. In one way or another moral fervour bedevilled theatre in Canada until well into the present century, but it was particularly damaging to the young and fragile theatre seeking to establish itself in the Atlantic provinces in the eighteenth and nineteenth centuries.

The Canadian debate about the moral value of drama was remarkable for its length and sincerity rather than for its depth and sophistication. Abuse, warnings, and sweeping generalizations about plays and players took precedence over rational argument: 'a Christian cannot with a safer Conscience enter into the Play-House than into a Brothel,' stormed the *Nova Scotia Chronicle and Weekly Advertiser* in January 1770. Such attacks were too persistent to be ignored: 'Theatricus', in the *Nova Scotia Gazette* (August 1768), pointed out that 'every great, wise, and polite Government, has ever with the Rise and Progress of the Arts, encouraged, and maintained Theatrical Amusements,' and argued that plays 'give entertaining Pictures of Mankind, convey a useful Lesson of Morality, and are an instructive School for Oratory.' A more pragmatic response was to use theatre for charitable purposes. From time to time proceeds from performances were specifically designated for charitable causes. Thus society was encouraged to extract some positive benefits from the production of plays, rather than to theorize about their moral value. In the *Royal Gazette and Nova Scotia Advertiser*, 21 January 1794, the Halifax Theatrical Society declared that 'all the profits which may arise . . . shall be paid into the Hands of the Church Wardens, who will faithfully and religiously apply the same to the relief of the indigent and distressed. . . .'

Despite—or, in part, because of—political and moral controversy theatre survived, even if Maritime communities sometimes had to endure lengthy spells with only sporadic dramatic entertainment. The moralists, however, were not the only threat to the development of Canadian drama. While garrisons and amateurs, whether permanent or temporary residents of Canada, were busy building theatres, acting in them, and even writing plays for them, professional companies, initially from the United States, were preparing to exploit the commercial possibilities of theatre in the Atlantic provinces—an attractive market in the eighteenth century when some eastern American states had suppressed theatre altogether. From very early on in English-

Canadian theatre history the stages were dominated by foreign professionals. The controversy surrounding the appointment of Englishman Peter Coe as artistic director of Edmonton's Citadel Theatre in 1977, and the even stormier row when another Englishman, John Dexter, was offered the directorship of the Stratford Festival in 1980, were remarkable only for the intense emotions they aroused. In other respects these appointments were no more than modern manifestations of common eighteenth- and nineteenth-century occurrences.

The first resident foreign professional company in Canada was probably the American Company of Comedians, which performed a Scottish tragedy (John Home's *Douglas*) and an English farce (David Garrick's *Miss in Her Teens*) in Halifax on 26 August 1768 and stayed for a fall season. Other American companies followed, including that of Addison B. Price, who organized seasons at the Fairbanks Wharf Theatre in Halifax in 1817 and 1818. And there is evidence of a visiting professional company in Saint John in 1799. A full record of such visits to Canada has yet to be compiled, but the pattern is reasonably clear. The Maritimes had an expanding population (Halifax's was over eight thousand in 1802), a demonstrated taste for theatre, and little professional capability of their own. Companies based in the United States, within manageable (though by no means easy) travelling distance from Halifax and Saint John, were ready to fill the gap. While Canadian audiences benefited from this in the sense that foreign professional companies could usually manage to present a more varied repertoire (consisting mostly of Shakespeare and English eighteenth-century comedy and tragedy) than garrison and amateur groups, a reliance on imported theatre reduced the necessity for the natural development of indigenous talent, thereby paving the way for commercial exploitation and cultural domination by American and British theatrical interests. The English actor E.A. Sothern, who appeared in Halifax several times between 1856 and 1859, contributed more to Canadian theatre than most visiting professionals. He co-operated with local amateur groups, produced a wide range of plays, brought celebrated actors with him, and refurbished the Spring Gardens theatre in the city. By his own admission, however—and naturally enough—he was in Halifax to 'coin money', not to cultivate a dramatic literature by Canadians or about Canada.

ONTARIO AND QUEBEC

As the drama struggled to establish itself in the Atlantic Provinces, significant developments were taking place in what is now Ontario. The War of 1812–14 and the Rebellion of 1837 indicated the need for a significant British military presence in Canada, and, as had happened in the Maritimes—and as would eventually happen in the West—garrisons in Lower and Upper Canada turned to theatricals in their leisure time. There is evidence of garrison performances in several Ontario cities, including York (Toronto), London, Ottawa, and Kingston as well as in Quebec City and Montreal. Sometimes the garrison put on its own shows (often for charitable purposes); sometimes the officers and men combined their talents with those of civilian amateurs and visiting professionals. These mixed bags of companies—undertrained, under-rehearsed, and performing on makeshift stages—impressed some audiences, disappointed others. One unenthusiastic spectator was an English businessman, John Lambert, whose grumpy reaction to some plays he saw in Lower Canada early in the nineteenth century perhaps reflected his failures in business (he made an unsuccessful attempt to set up a hemp industry in Canada) as much as the quality of the performance.

> There is, indeed, a building at Quebec called a Theatre, and also one at Montreal; but the persons who perform, or rather attempt to perform there, are as bad as the worst of our strolling actors; yet they have the conscience to charge the same price nearly as the London theatres. Sometimes the officers of the army lend their assistance to the company; but I have seen none, except Colonel Pye, and Captain Clark of the 49th, who did not murder the best scenes of our dramatic poets. It may be easily conceived how despicably low the Canadian theatricals must be, when boys are obliged to perform the female characters: the only actress being an old superannuated demirep, whose drunken Belvideras [in Thomas Otway's *Venice Preserved*, 1682], Desdemonas, and Isabellas, have often *enraptured* a Canadian audience.

Lambert's low opinion of most of the amateur actors he saw may have been justified, and he can hardly be blamed for objecting to drunkenness on stage. Nonetheless the overall picture of amateur theatricals in nineteenth-century Canada is not one of drunken incompetence but of enthusiasm, commitment, and no small degree of talent. Early nineteenth-century garrison and amateur productions—as is evident from John Lambert's description—favoured familiar British plays, often in uncongenial surroundings. The English actor John Bernard, for example, visited Quebec City in 1809 and had to act, according to his own description, 'in a paltry little room of a very paltry public-house, that neither in shape nor capacity merited the name of theatre.' In the same year an audience gathered in somewhat greater comfort in a Toronto ballroom to see Sheridan's *School for Scandal*. Maria L. Jarvis, daughter of the Secretary of Upper Canada, was present, and in a letter to her grandfather in New York she gave a brief account of the event. Unfortunately her breathless description of this first recorded dramatic performance in Toronto provides little firm detail of the 'theatre' in which it occurred. There is no doubt that it was rudimentary and temporary, but it seems to have been equipped with a pit and a gallery, and a reference by Miss Jarvis to 'York scandal hunters' suggests a fashionable audience. Other productions took place in upstairs rooms of inns and hotels or in 'Mr. Miller's Assembly-Room, formerly the Toronto Coffee House'. An advertisement in the *York Gazette*, 12 May 1810, for an entertainment here ends: 'Persons who honor the Exhibition with their company, need be under no apprehension of accidents by the future giving way of the Gallery, it having been secured under the direction of an obliging Gentleman.'

Even by mid-century, when purpose-built theatres were fairly plentiful, there was often cause for complaint. Sam Cowell, the leading comic singer of the American concert halls in the 1850s, ventured into Quebec and Ontario in 1860. His wife accompanied him and kept a detailed diary of their experiences. The Cowells, to put it mildly, were not impressed by things Canadian. Their two nights in Ottawa were particularly dismal, what with leaking gas, rats, and a swindling box-office keeper. In Niagara, Cowell had to compete with a dog fight for the audience's attention, and a yelping dog in Brantford caused similar problems. All in all, by the end of the tour Mrs Cowell was happy to leave Canada. 'It will,' she sighed, 'be quite a relief to get into a City like Detroit after these half savage villages.' Notwithstanding Mrs Cowell's preference for Detroit, Canada could boast some fine theatres by the middle of the nineteenth century. In addition to those in Halifax, Saint John, and other Maritime cities, Montreal built a theatre in 1804, and another, the New Montreal Theatre, seating 700 people, opened on 26 January 1818. The first two seasons ran for twenty-six and thirty-seven weeks respectively, until the theatre burned down on 4 May 1820. Other theatres in Montreal housed amateur and professional productions, and in 1825 John Molson built his splendid Theatre Royal, which cost some $30,000. A spacious building two stories high, with a Doric portico, it had two tiers of boxes, a pit, and a gallery. Located on the south-west corner of Saint-Paul and Victor, the theatre seated about 1,000. There were two dressing-rooms, a green room, a lobby, and other special rooms, and the decorations were of a high standard. Some Montrealers objected on principle to the opening of a new theatre in the city, but the general reaction was favourable. Under the management of Frederick Brown, an English actor who had appeared frequently in Montreal, the Theatre Royal opened on Monday 21 November 1825 with music, a prize address, Frederick Reynolds' comedy *The Dramatist*, and Isaac Bickerstaffe's farce, *The Spoiled Child*. Choruses of 'God Save the King' and 'Rule Britannia' helped keep the evening thoroughly British.

The Theatre Royal was demolished in 1844, but several new theatres opened in Montreal in the second half of the nineteenth century, including the Royal Olympic (1845), Hay's Theatre (1847), a new Theatre Royal (1852), the New Dominion (1873), the Academy of Music (1875), the Lyceum (1880), the Queen's (1891), and Her Majesty's (1898). No other city in Canada could match this record; only Toronto came close. Toronto's first important theatre—a converted Wesleyan Church—opened in 1834. Others followed, including the Royal Lyceum in 1848. Inveterate theatregoer George H. Ham, recalling his visits to the Lyceum as a young man, had no illusions about the theatre:

> The house was not at all gorgeous, nor was it outrageously clean. The mastication of tobacco, a popular method of enjoyment in those days, gave the floors, particularly in the gallery where the twenty-five centers assembled, a pattern and an odor not to be experienced in the modern theatres, where chewing gum is employed and indiscriminately parked.

But in 1872 the Lyceum was given a facelift. 'Toronto now possesses a theatre which in point of finish may compare favourably with any theatre of its size in the States or European continent,' boasted the *Mail* (24 August 1872).

Comfort, class segregation, aesthetic appeal, and technical proficiency were the desiderata of nineteenth-century Canadian theatres, and by the end of the century Ontario and Quebec had many theatres to be proud of. Toronto's Grand Opera House, reopened in 1879 after a fire destroyed the original (1874) building, accommodated an audience of 2,000, and London's Grand Opera House, with an even larger capacity, was much praised by European visitors. This elegant theatre was also destroyed by fire (in 1900), but the structure that replaced it maintained high standards of comfort and sophistication and is still operating as a major theatre in Ontario. Smaller cities and towns also found the resources to construct theatres. The 5,000 citizens of Gananoque, Ontario, could choose between two opera houses, each seating 1,000 spectators.

NINETEENTH-CENTURY DRAMA

Theatres in central Canada had changed beyond recognition from the 'paltry little room' that John Bernard complained about in 1809 to the splendours of opera houses on which little expense was spared. What had not changed very much, however, was the practice established by the early garrison theatres of presenting well-tried plays from abroad as the standard repertoire, usually under the auspices of visiting professional companies from Great Britain or the United States. Canadian box-office successes were not unheard of—indeed, one Canadian play, an adaptation of Gilbert Parker's novel, *The Seats of The Mighty*, was admired enough to achieve productions in Washington, New York, Boston, and London in 1896 and 1897, a pleasing reversal of the usual pattern. A romantic costume drama, *The Seats of the Mighty* is neither original nor inspiring, but at least it was stageable, which is more than can be said of the dramatic efforts of many of Parker's predecessors and contemporaries—mainly poetic dramatists whose achievements should be measured by quantity rather than quality. Murray Edwards discusses the poetic dramas of some twenty playwrights in *A Stage in our Past* and another critic, Michael Tait, has analysed in more detail the plays of Charles Heavysege, Charles Mair, and Wilfred Campbell. He concludes (with some justification) that 'Formlessness, ineffective characterization, pretentious moral attitudes, lack of stylistic distinction, stupefying prolixity, together with other unfortunate qualities vitiate most of the serious attempts at drama in Canada between 1860 and 1914.'

The tastes and ambitions of Canada's poetic dramatists varied. A few were interested in Canadian subjects, others looked to the Bible or to European history for their inspiration; some were keen to have their plays produced, others took no interest at all in the theatre; some chose the drama as their principal genre, while for others drama was merely an adjunct to their poetry. But all shared the ambition to write lofty plays with eternal themes, and all took themselves far too seriously.

Charles Heavysege, an Englishman who immigrated to Canada in 1853, had hopes that the American actress Charlotte Cushman would star in his biblical play, *Saul*. She died, however, before the plans were realized and *Saul* was never produced—though the play was published in 1857, was much admired by Hawthorne and Longfellow, and went through three editions. Hawthorne sent a copy of *Saul* to Coventry Patmore, who reviewed it in the Edinburgh and London periodical, the *North British Review* (vol. 29, 1858), finding in the play a 'quite startling' 'poetical power' and 'depth of psychological knowledge'. Northrop Frye, less impressed, places *Saul* in 'the tradition of the Victorian leviathan, the discursive poem combining a Biblical subject with middle-class morality.' At Patmore's suggestion Heavysege revised *Saul* for second and third editions (1859, 1868), but no significant improvement is discernible. It is remarkable that Patmore found such merit in the play; it is turgid and long-winded, not unlike Heavysege's other play, *Count Filippo* (1860), a tragicomedy morality play about marriage. (CBC Radio bravely broadcast adaptations of *Count Filippo* and *Saul* in 1968 and 1973 respectively.)

Charles Mair, a native Canadian, was a leading member of the 'Canada First' movement, and the poetic drama *Tecumseh*, his best-known work, shows it. First published in 1886, the play deals with the War of 1812 and has strong chauvinistic inclinations. 'As the play of *Henry V* was a song of triumph to the English of Shakespeare's time, so is this a song of triumph for the Canadians of today,' trumpeted the *Globe* (20 February 1886). Mair himself thought *Tecumseh* 'a good acting play . . . for it is full of striking situations—I may live to see it on the boards in Toronto yet.' Although both Toronto Truck Theatre and Factory Theatre (also in Toronto) staged versions in the early 1970s, the play, despite occasional dramatic tension, is virtually unactable. Mair shows little sense of the realities of the stage, and his determination to write anti-American propaganda stifles the creative impulses that sometimes suggest there is life in the play. However, like *Saul, Tecumseh* was widely acclaimed when it was published and a second edition was called for in 1901.

This edition contains a revealing preface in which Mair explains his laudable intention to create 'an original and distinctive literature' for Canada, an intention that was echoed by another well-intentioned but inept verse dramatist, Sarah Anne Curzon. Curzon was as determined as Mair to define a Canadian mythology. In her *Laura Secord, the Heroine of 1812* (1887) the War of 1812 again provides the setting. But again—as in *Tecumseh*—patriotic enthusiasm is no recipe for compelling drama. Curzon recreates the Laura Secord legend, but excessively long speeches, a lack of dramatic tension, shallow characterization, and cloying sentimentality destroy the play. However, Curzon's short prose comedy, *The Sweet Girl Graduate*, published in the periodical *Grip-Sack* in 1882, is an engaging play, adroitly attacking sexual discrimination in the University of Toronto.

Curzon wrote only two plays. Wilfred Campbell, born in Berlin, Ontario, in 1858, was a prolific playwright, but not a better one, and he had little interest in Canadian heroes. He wrote historical verse dramas; none were performed, but four were published: *Mordred*, *Hildebrand*, *Daulac*, and *Morning*, collected in *Poetical Tragedies* (1908). To his credit Campbell took some interest in live theatre; Carl F. Klinck has described him as 'a student and observer of stage tactics and strategy, artistically sensitive to dramatic effects.' Campbell hoped that *Mordred* might be produced, perhaps by Henry Irving, but to no avail. For Michael Tait, 'Campbell's personality is not attractive. The modern reader is repelled by his lack of humour, his provincialism, pretentiousness and purblind Anglophobia.' His plays, Tait continues, are marred by 'artificial diction, insecure grammar, grotesque rhythms. . . .' Some understanding of Campbell's failure can be gained from an essay he published in the *Canadian Magazine* in November 1907, 'Shakespeare and the Latter-Day Drama'. In defending Shakespeare against modern playwrights, Campbell betrays a slavish addiction to British culture: 'any one who prefers the general character of the Ibsen or Bernard Shaw play to that of Shakespeare is welcome to his opinion, but his mental attitude is scarcely one which will conduce to the development of the best ideals of the British race.'

In the 1840s Eliza Lanesford Cushing published in a major Canadian literary journal, the *Literary Garland*, several short plays and dramatic fragments on Biblical or historical subjects. Cushing's only full-length play, *Esther, a Sacred Drama* (1840), ponderously depicts the trials and tribulations of Jewish Queen Esther in King Ahasuerus's Persia. The blank verse of *Esther* is as stilted as that in John Hunter Duvar's *The Enamorado* (1879), set in fifteenth-century Spain, and in his *De Roberval* (1888), though *De Roberval* has a mildly interesting plot concerning religious and cultural conflict between the French and the Indians in Quebec in the 1840s. Thomas Bush's verse melodrama, *Santiago* (1866), is a gothic South American extravaganza that is hard to take seriously, with its unconvincing Byronic hero, implausible incidents, and unspeakable verse.

Self-consciously literary, detached from the theatrical realities that only live performance can provide, and distracted by foreign models, Canada's poetic playwrights succeeded only in satisfying themselves and a few of their literary peers. Like their counterparts in England and the United States, they left no mark on the mainstream of amateur or professional theatre of their time.

It is refreshing to turn from these arid poetic dramas to plays that found a place in the repertoire of Canada's nineteenth-century theatres. Many original Canadian farces, comic operas, and melodramas were written and produced in the nineteenth century, and they offered audiences an alternative to the standard British fare favoured by the relentless touring companies from Great Britain and the United States. Admittedly, the melodramas of W.A. Tremayne, the most popular of Canadian playwrights of the late nineteenth and early twentieth centuries, are refreshing only in comparison with the poetic dramas of his contemporaries. Tremayne's plays were stageworthy, and occasionally he made an effort to create a Canadian context for his plots—as in *The Black Feather*, for instance, produced at Toronto's Grand Opera House on 8 September 1916 (and published in Boston in 1918 as *The Man Who Went*). But Tremayne's success, in Canada and the United States, was built not on artistic imagination but on a rather routine ability to provide hackneyed romantic and melodramatic vehicles for American stars, such as Robert Mantell, who appeared in Tremayne's adaptation (unpublished) of Joseph Hatton's novel *The Dagger and the Cross* in Toronto in March 1900.

More imaginative (and more whimsical) than the efforts of Tremayne are the plays of Frederick Augustus Dixon. Unlike the commercially minded Tremayne, Dixon enjoyed vice-regal patronage, and his plays were frequently performed at Government House, Ottawa. Titles such as *Fifine, the Fisher-Maid; or, The Magic Shrimps* (published in Ottawa in 1877, and performed at Government House on 1 January 1878) and *Maiden Mona the Mermaid* (published in Toronto in 1877, and performed at Government House on 1 January 1877) hardly inspire confidence, but these comic fantasies do manage to incorporate a variety of amusing satirical allusions to current topics and personalities. Naturally, for a playwright enjoying the patronage of the British aristocracy, Dixon's works stress imperialist values. Just as Lescarbot's masque of 1606 had celebrated French imperial power, so, for example, Dixon's masque, *Canada's Welcome*, celebrates the benevolence of imperial England. First performed before Governor General the Marquis of Lorne and his wife (the Princess Louise) at the Grand Opera House in Ottawa on 24 February 1879, the masque unfolds:

> *and, to the sound of music, there entered a procession, emblematic of the history of Canada, having therein certain dressed in the costumes of those nations whose people have hewn down her forests and built up her cities. At the last come those who should represent the divers Provinces in Confederation; and these, advancing to the tree where Canada lay concealed, drew her forth, and placed upon her a noble vestment and a wealth of golden maple leaves.*

Dixon's characterization of the provinces is interesting: Ontario, a female figure in a white dress, wears a head-dress of '*autumnal maple leaves and corn, emblematic of her agricultural wealth*'; Prince Edward Island is a '*sturdy farmer*'; British Columbia is a miner, '*a revolver being in his belt, and having a pick on his shoulder and a bag of gold in his hand*'; New Brunswick is a lady '*wearing water lilies in her hair*'; Manitoba, a trapper, and Nova Scotia, a fisherman, sing a charming duet in praise of their occupations. Quebec is seen as 'quaint' and in need of English protection:

> I, Quebec, am come with greeting;
> With the grace of other days;
> Bringing to our happy meeting
> Quaint and curious bygone ways.
> ....
> Long may England's mighty lions
> Guard the *fleurs de lys* of France.

The only discordant note is in the opening speech of the masque when an Indian chief laments the loss of his country: 'The Manitou has spoken! From the distant east / Rises the dawn; the dawn that brings us death.' As he speaks, Canada enters, '*robed as an Indian maiden*'.

A happy contrast to the cloying conservatism of *Canada's Welcome* is found in the many early Canadian farces and satires that drew energy and authenticity from an involvement with local and national issues. The texts of plays such as *The Female Consistory of Brockville* (1856), *Dolorsolatio* (1865), *The Fair Grit* (1876), *H.M.S. Parliament* (1880), and *Ptarmigan* (1895) are now, fortunately, easily available in the four-volume collection of *Canada's Lost Plays* (1978–82), edited by Anton Wagner. The strength of these plays lies in their lively personal, social, and political satire, and in their eminent stageworthiness—*Dolorsolatio*, *H.M.S. Parliament*, and *Ptarmigan*, for example, enjoyed successful productions in major theatres (Montreal's Theatre Royal, Montreal's Academy of Music, and Hamilton's Grand Opera House, respectively).

The Female Consistory of Brockville, by an unknown author self-styled as 'Caroli Candidus', satirizes high-minded and hypocritical Presbyterian women who have ousted their minister on a false charge; based on an actual Brockville situation, the play also attacks corruption in the church and the law. The prose, and the occasional verse, are rich in rhythm and imagery and are refreshingly free of the forced rhetoric that characterizes most nineteenth-century poetic drama. Lady Mulish, declares her father-in-law, is 'a walking epitime [sic] of imposture, as ignorant as a Hottentot, as forward as a dragon, as vain as a peacock, as fierce as a pole-cat, and with a tongue like the tails o' Samson's foxes.' Sir George Mulish is a finely drawn study of a henpecked husband who perverts the law in order to please his wife. The deposed minister who dominates the play's action appears only in the fine surrealistic conclusion where the traditional male/female conflict is given mythic overtones as his 'corpse' rises from the bier to scatter the women who, Maenad-like, dance ritualistically as they chant:

> His blood on us will leave no stain.
> But look how he laughs!
> And the free air quaffs!
> We've struck his head, we've struck his heart,
> Expended all our female art,
> But still his life will not depart,—
> For see—he laughs!

Dolorsolatio, 'a local political burlesque' by pseudonymous Sam Scribble, author of other farces performed and published in Montreal in the mid–1860s, is a pro-Confederation sketch whose construction shows an experienced sense of the theatre, combining dialogue, chorus, dance, music, burlesque, tableaux, and skilful use of a trapdoor and lighting effects. The characters include Grandpapa Canada, Master East ('a gentleman of French education'), and Master West ('younger son of Canada, an overgrown boy'), who embody French and English cultural differences and whose quarrels are further developed in the rivalry between Montreal ('a fashionable young lady') and Toronto ('a young lady with a very good opinion of herself'):

> MONTREAL: Who Grandpapa, without of doubt a particle,
> I, Montreal, am *the* superior article!
> TORONTO: You're well enough—in many ways you shine—
> But your appearance don't come up to mine—
> MONTREAL: Appearance! yours! I laugh at such
> pretence—*I've* got the *Dollars*!
> TORONTO: And I've got *the sense*!

The play's comic conflicts touch on such contemporary issues as transportation ('Dat Grand Tronk Railway is so goddam slow'), federal inefficiency ('*Ottawa tries to build, but the bricks always fall down*'), and language differences ('I never could a-bear them *parlez-vous*!'). The rivalry between Eastern Canada and Western Canada and between Montreal and Toronto is contrasted with the fight between Mr Abe North and Mr Jefferson South (the American Civil War) who are ordered out by Grandpapa Canada. 'Not in my house! I won't have such marauders / Spoiling my garden, trampling on my borders!'

Faced with the dangerous example of a secessionist South, Santa Claus offers the feuding provinces medicine from a demijohn labelled DOLORSOLATIO.

> DOLORSOLATIO! would you like to taste!
> This remedy is new, but most expedient!
> And 'Federation' is the sole ingredient!

Nicholas Flood Davin's *The Fair Grit* adopts a less optimistic view of the Canadian political situation than that offered in *Dolorsolatio*. Born in Ireland in 1840, Davin had a colourful career in Canada as a journalist, poet, lawyer, and Tory Member of Parliament for Assiniboia (his career in the West was the subject of Ken Mitchell's 1979 play, *Davin: the Politician*). Taking a love affair between Angelina (the 'fair grit') and George (a Tory) as its central situation, the play exposes the divisiveness of party politics and the venality of politicians. Davin terms his play a 'farce', but it also has a powerful satiric edge voiced most strongly through the persona of Ronald, '*a cynic given to express himself strongly*':

> They [the politicians] out-vie each other first in professions of purity, and then out-do each other, as far as it is possible, in acts of corruption. . . . In Opposition all is virtue; in power all the reverse.

And some of Ronald's pronouncements have an uncanny timeliness: 'We have ministers talking like children about political economy—a science they never studied, and if they had, they couldn't have mastered it. We have persons who don't know its rudiments thoroughly, dogmatizing about free trade, as if any man of mark ever held that free trade was applicable to the condition of every country. . . .' Although *The Fair Grit* is occasionally weighed down by ponderous politicizing and opaque political allusion, it just as often sparkles with aphorisms and compelling theatricality—scene two, for example, is an effective exposé of nineteenth-century electioneering.

There is further political exploration in *Ptarmigan; or, A Canadian Carnival*, a comic opera by Jean Newton McIlwraith, with music by J.E.P. Aldous. A Canadian who becomes an American citizen is defended on grounds of temporary insanity, and redeems himself by tearing up his American naturalization papers. This anti-annexation theme is, however, tempered by the quiet reflection that 'the same trees grow on either side of the Niagara River, the same birds sing, the same flowers bloom. . . .' And McIlwraith has little sympathy for Canadian nationalism. She mocks a chorus of girls who hypocritically profess cultural and economic independence of the United States:

> Every novel that we read's a home production,
> Every play we go to see's Canadian,
> Every native work we buy—at a reduction,
> Every local horse we bet on—if we can.
> Oh, we never get a costume from abroad,
> To Detroit for our shopping never go;
> And we boldly plead not guilty of a fraud,
> Such as smuggling Yankee boots from Buffalo.

McIlwraith's ideal, it transpires, is Canadian allegiance to Britain. Hepatica, the play's 'herald', asks, 'Is it possible to conceive of anyone, man or woman, in full possession of his or her senses, deliberately renouncing his or her British birthright and electing to become amalgamated with the mobocracy upon our southern boundary?'

Ptarmigan is not particularly inventive, and even the best of the nineteenth-century satires—William Henry Fuller's *H.M.S. Parliament*—owes a good deal to Gilbert and Sullivan's *H.M.S. Pinafore* for its plot, music, and lyrics. *H.M.S. Parliament*'s theme and satire, however, are entirely Canadian, and Fuller handles his material with great versatility. The satire is directed principally at Sir John A. Macdonald, his ministers, and their policies—particularly the National Policy ('N.P.'),which restricted free trade and caused rising prices— and there are many hits against corruption in politics, an area with which Macdonald was not unfamiliar, and against the Civil Service. The Prime Minister appears in *H.M.S. Parliament* as the rather unimaginatively named Capt. Mac.A. Other identifiable political figures are Thomas Black, M.P. for Cardwell, Ontario, who has a taste for ginger pop 'with the old rye flavour' (he actually worked for many years on behalf of the Sons of Temperance), Alexander Mackenzie, the former Prime Minister ('Alexander MacDeadeye'), and Sir Samuel Tilley, the Minister of Finance ('Sir Samuel Sillery'). 'Ben Burr' is the self-styled poet-laureate Josiah Burr Plumb, M.P. for Niagara. The roles of the young lovers, Sam Sniffer and Angelina, remain fresh and unhackneyed partly because Fuller uses them to guy the conventions of Victorian courtship, and partly because Sam is something of a tippler and ne'er-do-well, while Angelina is a worldly-wise young lady. ('To elope, to marry, to marry, ay; there's the rub, / For, if we marry, what have we to live on . . . ?') The work is well crafted with a number of fine comic scenes, such as one where Angelina tries to teach the pompous Sir Samuel to dance the 'Boston'. The closing scene is in the nature of an epilogue, with Canada attempting to convince mother Britannia that she has not been more spendthrift than her sisters, New Zealand and Australia, in building a railway to enable Britannia to visit her 'dear children all the way off in British Columbia!' *H.M.S. Parliament* also raises an issue common to so many works of the period—Canadian/U.S. relations.

> BRITANNIA: . . . . I am told you are carrying on a flirtation with your 'Cousin Jonathan,' and some people are even talking about an alliance between you. *Reproachfully.* Oh! Canada, *I would never have believed it of a well-conducted girl like you*!
> CANADA: *Indignantly. It's a horrid story mamma.* I like 'Jonathan' very much as a near neighbour and a cousin, but I should never dream of a closer connection, and I don't believe he desires it either. . . .

First staged by the American producer E.A. McDowell in Montreal on 16 February 1880, *H.M.S. Parliament* was acted in many Canadian cities in 1880. Thereafter its popularity declined—inevitably, in view of its topicality—but it enjoyed a successful revival in a 1983 University of Toronto production.

Fuller wrote another political satire, *The Unspecific Scandal*, first published in the *Canadian Illustrated News* in January 1874. This satire, an attack on Macdonald and his involvement in the Pacific Railway Scandal, seems never to have been produced. Plays and dramatic sketches by other writers were published in the *Illustrated News* and periodicals such as *Grip* and the *Literary Garland*. They were also frequently published anonymously by publishing houses in Toronto, Ottawa, Montreal, and even New York and Chicago, and were not normally intended for production. Anton Wagner lists close to two hundred nineteenth-century titles in *The Brock Bibliography of Published Canadian Plays in English 1766–1978*, and Patrick O'Neill adds more in a checklist published in 1982 and 1983. A relatively small number of these plays were produced; on the other hand, plays were produced that were never published. Toronto theatre manager John Nickinson, for example, staged the first Canadian play to be seen in Toronto, *Fiddle, Faddle and Foozle*, a farce by George Simcoe Lee, on 9 April 1853, and another Lee play, *Saucy Kate*, premièred on 11 July of the same year, followed on 13 January 1854 by a play by Nickinson himself, *The Fortune of War*.

All these plays—produced or unproduced—attest to the growth of a playwriting tradition in central Canada in the nineteenth century. The interests of the playwrights were, of course, shaped and conditioned by the values of the society for which they wrote, and although Canadian dramatists and theatre managers did not have to suffer the systematic censorship system (through the licensing of plays) that had long been established in Great Britain, they were not free from restraints and pressures. Libel laws and cautious theatre managers kept political satire under control, and a general skepticism in some powerful segments of society—particularly the church—deterred the theatre from promoting strongly radical or reformist ideas.

AUDIENCES

From the beginning of professional theatre in Canada audiences were drawn from a wide social range. Performances at Frank's Hotel in Toronto in 1825 were attended not only by 'gentlemen and ladies of rank and fashion, peers, parliament men, placemen, cabinet ministers, and other ministers', but also by 'barristers' clerks, attorneys' apprentices, shopkeepers, with an editor or two' (*York Colonial Advocate*, 29 December 1825). Ticket prices fluctuated considerably, depending on a company's ability to attract audiences. Even late into the nineteenth century it was possible to buy a gallery ticket for a dime in Montreal or Toronto. Whereas audiences at garrisons, at Rideau Hall, or at other amateur productions tended to be restricted to the middle and upper classes, the professional theatre was within the reach of virtually everyone. The variety of people attending the theatre was matched by the variety of reasons they had for being there. Seeing a play was only one reason. As public places, theatres were excellent venues for expressing feelings and opinions. A Montreal audience in 1811, for example, made a firm political point to some Americans who refused to remove their hats during the playing of the national anthem. Violence resulted, as the *Canadian Courant* reported on 4 February 1811:

> It is so customary in all British Theatres for the Band to play *God save the King!* at least *once in the course of the evening*, during which the audience are uncovered—we earnestly recommend to the gentlemen from the United States who visit our Theatre, to comply with the established custom. But we cannot perceive the propriety of allowing a number of boys and tumultuous persons in the Pit to assail *Strangers* in the manner we have lately witnessed, with sticks and canes, for the purpose of compelling their compliance.

In order to suppress incidents of this sort, as well as to control sundry drunks who sometimes disrupted proceedings, police were often present in nineteenth-century Canadian theatres. But even when present they were sometimes powerless against mob violence. When Edmund Falconer's *Peep o'Day; or, Savourneen Deelish* was produced in Montreal in 1862 the audience objected to some religious incidents, and the offending actor, Charles Fisher—after having been pelted on stage with apples, turnips, and eggs—was attacked, according to Montreal theatre historian Franklin Graham, by a mob of five hundred outside the theatre. Fisher escaped serious injury by hiding in a private house.

One might think that tumult and violence were caused by ignorant philistines, of whatever class. But that was not always the case. Toronto students, for example, could behave very boorishly in the theatre. The English actor E.S. Willard, performing with his company in Henry Arthur Jones's *Judah* at the Grand Opera House (on one of his tours in the early 1890s), was forced to stop the play when students in the gallery disrupted it by shying programs (folded into darts) at actors and audience, accompanied by a chorus of what critic Hector Charlesworth described as 'weird noises'. On the other hand, when Sarah Bernhardt acted in Montreal in 1880 she found the enthusiasm of students much to her liking.

Some of the most attentive and appreciative audiences were those who preferred vaudeville and burlesque houses to legitimate theatres. The shows put on at houses like the Star in Toronto were a favourite target of the moralists; but regardless of the content of the show, audiences there seem to have been as well, if not better, behaved than those at allegedly more respectable theatres. On 7 February 1903 *Saturday Night* published an account by an unsympathetic reporter of an evening at the Star—'Here is an opportunity for some clergyman or social reformer looking for something to reform'—but despite his obvious distaste for that night's strip-tease show (he watched it all most attentively) he found no disorder in the behaviour of an 'exacting audience'.

It is difficult to generalize about audiences, especially over a large time span. Geographical location, economic conditions, management policy, the type of theatre, and many other factors can influence the nature of an audience at any given time. A few observations, however, seem worth offering. Professional theatre in central Canada in the nineteenth century maintained its appeal to virtually all classes of society; audiences increased in size as theatres and opera houses were built to accommodate them; their tastes ran the gamut from burlesque to Shakespeare; they could be, and frequently were, rowdy, sometimes violently so; they enjoyed theatre, and freely voiced their enjoyment—at least until a deadening middle-class sense of propriety modified their behaviour and left only the blandness we are accustomed to today. Audiences also became increasingly conservative in their tastes, reluctant to accept innovation in dramatic form or content. While standard melodramas were nearly always sure of a warm welcome, Ibsen and Shaw—on the rare occasions their plays were performed—were greeted with hostility or bewilderment.

EARLY THEATRE IN WESTERN CANADA

Canada's climate and geography, with their extremes of temperature and distance, have always impeded development of theatre, and nowhere more so than in the West. Theatre in Western Canada also struggled against a small population base and a fair share of Victorian anti-theatrical prejudice. The arguments rehearsed throughout the Maritimes, Quebec, and Ontario in the eighteenth and nineteenth centuries duly travelled West to dog the theatre there. An 1883 sermon by Winnipeg's Reverend J.B. Silcox (published in the *Winnipeg Daily Times*, 19 February 1883), while more rational and less rhetorical than was customary at the time, still argued that theatre 'has sinned against morality and decency.' In the United States, 'the devil and hell' had been let loose in theatres, and in Toronto 'within the last few years, there were scenes on the boards that would cause even the Sodomites to blush, and stop their ears for shame.' However, the church, of whatever denomination, was no more able to prevent the establishment of theatre in the West than it had been elsewhere in Canada. But the church was not the theatre's only enemy. Even segments of society that professed support for the cultural and social benefits provided by theatre balked as some *kinds* of theatres. An interesting case in point is the Winnipeg theatre critic C.W. Handscomb of the *Manitoba Free Press*. A playwright as well as a critic, and a friend of theatre manager C.P. Walker, Handscomb did a great deal to encourage the growth of theatre in Winnipeg, but when Ibsen's *Ghosts* came to town in March 1904 he turned decidedly cantankerous. As a drama critic, he seems to have sensed an unusual achievement, finding *Ghosts*, 'from a dramatic standpoint', to be 'remarkably strong'. The moralist, however, takes precedence. Obviously upset by Ibsen's delving into such an unsavoury subject as venereal disease, Handscomb worried that this 'unwholesome, degrading [and] disgusting' play might pollute the 'wholesome prairie atmosphere'.

> The audacious daring with which sex questions are discussed in this play has no stage precedent—not even the risqué problem plays have gone so far—while the utter depravity of the characters is astounding.
> There are only half a dozen of these characters, but there doesn't appear to be a redeeming trait in one of them. They are all morally diseased—bad when the play begins and at the limit of brazen sinfulness by the time it ends. . . .

The 1907 Canadian première of Shaw's *Mrs Warren's Profession* (which had been suppressed in New York and the cast arrested) occasioned some gripping hyperbole from 'E.B.' in the *Manitoba Free Press* on 1 May 1907. 'No more unwholesome nor repulsive play has ever been seen in Winnipeg,' he wrote. 'It has not one redeeming feature. . . . The play is a beatification of evil living, a sermon on the advantages of vice, and the story of a woman whom to term a courtesan would be a compliment.' *Mrs Warren's Profession* closed after one performance, giving way to a piece more acceptable to Winnipeg tastes: 'Cowboys, cowgirls, United States cavalry men,

Mexicans, senoras and senoritas, and a ''tenderfoot'' will make up the motley gathering in Richard Carle's great musical comedy success, *The Tenderfoot*. . . .' (*Free Press*, 1 May 1907).

Despite the moral outrage expressed by preachers and critics, Western Canadians in the nineteenth century were keen theatregoers. As was the case elsewhere in Canada, the social mix, values, and behaviour of Western audiences varied, although it may be that on the whole there was rather less gentility and propriety, and correspondingly more rowdiness and violence in Western theatres than in those of Central and Eastern Canada.

The presence of prostitutes caused disturbances from time to time, even when they were cordoned off from the rest of the audience, as was the practice, for example, at Winnipeg's Princess Theatre in the 1880s. More serious, however, was the riot caused by racial segregation at the Colonial Theatre in Victoria in 1860. As reported in the *British Colonist* (6 November 1860), two negroes insisted on being admitted to the parquet, or stalls, an area reserved for whites only. White members of the audience objected to this threat to their privileges and fighting broke out. At one point a negro was set on fire by a camphene lamp thrown at him. The rioting was eventually subdued by police intervention. The extent of turbulence in Western Canadian theatres should, however, be kept in proportion; audiences at Winnipeg's Walker Theatre or Vancouver's Opera House could behave as decorously as any in Toronto or Montreal.

In Western Canada the history of theatre buildings from the earliest theatrical performances in British Columbia in the 1850s to, say, the opening of the new Regina Theatre in 1910, reveals impressive variety. A contemporary account by Frances Herring points out that one of the first public buildings erected in New Westminster was a 'squaw dance-house', as well as 'other places of amusement for the passing throng', including a theatre 'in the shape of an extended wooden shack' at the back of a hotel. Extended or not, wooden shacks as theatres leave much to be desired. The semblance of a recognizable theatre was not long in coming—Victoria's Colonial Theatre opened on 4 February 1860—but unusual performance spaces prevailed prior to and after the building of the Colonial. As in the Maritimes, the military led the way. Professional and amateur productions in Victoria were mounted in the 1850s in temporary facilities, such as a converted room in the city's Royal Hotel, and garrison plays could be seen at Fort Victoria. But the British navy was responsible for arranging the first European theatrical event in British Columbia, which took place on board *H.M.S. Trincomalee* in Esquimalt Harbour on 18 October 1853. No detailed account of the occasion survives, but accounts of later naval theatricals of the same kind (in the *Daily Colonist*, 26 February 1863, for example) show that the officers and men were capable of organizing an entertaining evening of theatre for their guests from on shore, by erecting a proscenium stage for plays and songs, and providing ample refreshments and comfort.

Creating theatre in the absence of conventional theatre facilities became a Western virtue. While virtue is not a quality normally associated with the Klondike gold rush, that madcap enterprise nevertheless shows how important theatre has been in Canadian society. The theatrical boom that accompanied the gold rush in Dawson City lasted only a couple of years, but Michael Booth has called it 'the most sensational and flamboyant period in the history of Canadian theatre.' The pages of Dawson's newspaper, the *Klondike Nugget*, provide abundant evidence to support this view, as do the many reminiscences of Klondike prospectors. Dawson City's theatres appeared and disappeared (often by fire) as rapidly as fortunes were made and lost. Impressive names—the Opera House, the Pavilion, the Monte Carlo, the Orpheum—concealed rudimentary, hastily constructed facilities. The theatres were unlike any others in Canada, before or since: multi-purpose buildings used for gambling, drinking, and dancing, as well as for theatrical productions. A typical evening's entertainment was a mixed-bag affair offering a wide assortment of attractions, but usually including a play of some sort, as well as vaudeville acts, song-and-dance routines, and wrestling and boxing matches. Plays were also mounted in the Chautauqua tents that criss-crossed Western Canada throughout the 1920s and early '30s. Theatrical fare in this Methodist-inspired educational movement usually consisted of unsullied comedies or melodramas, or classics such as Sheridan's *The Rivals*, described in a 1921 Chautauqua program as 'clean, wholesome humor from start to finish'.

Writing in the *Canadian Magazine* in May 1908, Frederic Robson suggested that 'as most people who have travelled through the West know, the theatres of the plains and through the mountains are not generally the lovely creatures we have in Toronto and Montreal, and the travelling actor from Fort William westward must put up with inconvenience of no light order.' Inconveniences there certainly were. The 'theatre' in Emerson, Manitoba, for example, in the 1880s, according to Franklin Graham, 'was an old warehouse full of farming implements and boxes. The place had but two exits, one of which was from the platform to the prairie, where tents had been rigged up for the company [of Charles Arnold]. There was not a house nearer than a mile, and, as everybody came on horseback, the outside was like a horse fair. Soap and candle boxes formed the back seats, champagne and brandy cases being in front.' Accounts of poor facilities in theatres in Western Canada are legion, and are not entirely figments of the prejudiced imagination of easterners. But such accounts must be balanced by a recognition that the West, in many cases, achieved a high degree of sophistication in theatre design, construction, and furnishings.

Vancouver's first theatre, Hart's Opera House, was a flimsy wooden structure that had originally been a roller-skating rink. But the Vancouver Opera House, built by the CPR for some $100,000, and opened in February 1891, was a different matter. Seating over 1,200 people, the theatre enjoyed the most modern equipment and accommodations, and mounted an elaborate opening-night production of *Lohengrin*, with opera star Emma Juch. Nevertheless, the Vancouver Opera House was outclassed by what remains in many ways the most impressive theatre ever constructed in Western Canada—Winnipeg's Walker Theatre. Built in 1907 by theatre magnate C.P. Walker, and now operating as a movie house, the theatre was considered by Walker's daughter (Ruth Harvey) to be 'simple' and 'functional'. Liberally supplied with ivory and marble, and with a seating capacity of close to 2,000, it was, in fact, far from being merely simple and functional. (Such epithets are more properly applied to theatres like the Opera House in Hanley, Saskatchewan, opened in 1914, with its kerosene lamps and kitchen chairs.) Only seven years old when the Walker Theatre opened, Ruth Harvey grew to know her father's theatre intimately. In her memoirs she waxes eloquent about the Edwardian decoration, the marbled lobby with its 'huge chandelier of beaded glass', and the 'crimson plush' of the seats in the auditorium.

Though Regina, a smaller city than Winnipeg, could not afford a theatre like the Walker, there was nothing shabby about the new theatre (named the Regina Theatre) that opened in Saskatchewan's capital in February 1910—not Regina's first, but certainly its best to that point in the city's history. Elegant, well-equipped, and commodious, it was described in the *Regina Morning Leader*, 5 February 1910, as a small-scale 'replica' of the Walker Theatre, and 'without exception . . . the finest of its kind between Winnipeg and the Pacific coast'.

> . . . The stage is 30 feet deep, 57 feet wide; height of grid 44 feet and is only one foot shallower than the largest theatre in Minneapolis. . . . Dressing room accommodation has been made for 80 people, fitted up in comfortable manner. The proscenium arch rises from the ground floor some 20 feet in height.
>
> In the house proper, seating accommodation has been carefully looked after. There are eight boxes and altogether 850 people can be seated. The parquet will hold 500 persons with wide and direct aisles with leather cushioned chairs set on steps so that a clear view can be seen from every part of the house, the slope being one in twelve. The balcony holds 350 and is curved round to meet the upper boxes. Two large five foot stairways lead from the foyer to the balcony. . . . The front of the building contains entrance lobby, box office, cloakroom, ladies' toilet, while in the basement a gentlemen's smoking room is to be found. . . .
>
> The exterior is executed in Roman bluff pressed brick and Tyndall stone, giving a very appropriate and unique facade.

The remarkable thing is not so much that a small prairie city like Regina (population 30,000 in 1911) supported such an elegant theatre, but that in the context of late nineteenth- and early twentieth-century theatrical development in Western Canada there was nothing exceptional about Regina's achievement. Theatre was extremely important to communities large and small in the West. This is made clear in the pages of *Julius Cahn's Official Theatrical Guide* (commonly known as *Cahn's Guide*), which was published from 1896 to 1920, and was the most authoritative source of statistical information about American and Canadian theatres of the period for booking agents and producers who were taking shows on the road.

By the outbreak of the First World War, Western Canada had the theatres and the audiences to sustain widespread theatrical activity. It is important to consider as well the kind of plays—and the companies that presented them—likely to be available for these theatres and audiences. Both plays and companies were predominantly foreign. The topic of foreign touring companies is taken up later, but a useful survey of the situation as it affected one representative Western Canadian city—Edmonton—can be given here.

The souvenir program for the opening of Edmonton's New Empire Theatre in 1920 contained—besides a description of the theatre—an account, 'Fifteen Years of Edmonton Theatre Going', by A.B. Watt. Over this fifteen-year span (1905–1920) Watt and other Edmontonians had the opportunity of seeing all manner of theatrical entertainment, from vaudeville to opera. Though Watt was an enthusiastic rather than a discriminating theatregoer, his reminiscences are valuable both for the information they provide and for the sense of excitement they convey. He singles out for comment performances by the Roscian Opera Company, the Juvenile Bostonians, Harold Nelson's Canadian stock company and its offerings of Shakespearean plays, Mrs Minnie Fiske's visit in July 1907, when she played in Langdon Mitchell's *The New York Idea*, and her return with her company in 1919 in *Mis' Nelly of N'Orleans*. Other visitors included George Arliss, Emily Stevens, John Mason, Jeanne Russell, and Willard Mack, as well as Shakespearean actors such as Sir Johnstone Forbes-Robertson, Robert B. Mantell (who came three times), John E. Kellerd, and Canadian actress Margaret Anglin, who came on four occasions and played in *Twelfth Night*, *As You Like It*, and *The Taming of the Shrew* in November 1913. In May 1914 Sir Frank Benson was in Edmonton with his Stratford-on-Avon players. Watt terms 1913 Edmonton's *annus mirabilis*, for in that year Sarah Bernhardt played one act of *Camille* at the Orpheum opposite the French actor Lou Tellegen (who later married the famous opera singer Geraldine Farrar), Maude Adams appeared in Barrie's *Peter Pan*, and Forbes-Robertson in Jerome K. Jerome's *The Passing of The Third Floor Back*. In January 1914 the Quinlan Opera Company presented *Tannhauser*, *Tales of Hoffman*, *Faust*, and *Madame Butterfly* (in English), and the famous San Carlo Opera Company performed in Edmonton on three subsequent occasions. In March and April 1914 Sir John Martin-Harvey, sponsored by the British-Canadian Theatrical Organization, appeared in *The Only Way*, an adaptation of Dickens' *A Tale of Two Cities* by Freeman Wills and Canon Langbridge, *The Breed of the Treshams* by John Rutherford, and *The Cigarette Maker's Romance* by Charles Hannan. Sir Henry Irving's son Laurence Irving, and his wife Mabel Hackney, who was Irving *père*'s former leading lady, played Edmonton in the spring of 1914, only a few weeks before they both drowned in the sinking of the *Empress of Ireland* in the St Lawrence River. Watt felt that the evening of 13 February 1915, when Forbes-Robertson appeared as Hamlet, was 'the greatest in Edmonton's theatrical history'.

Watt also draws attention to a 1918 touring production of Somerset Maugham's play *The Land of Promise*, which was set partly in Canada, identifying it confusingly as 'the only Canadian play that has ever been presented here with a genuine Canadian flavor'. It is ironic, but not surprising, that Edmontonians had to rely on a British playwright for 'Canadian' drama. Dominated, as Watt shows, by imported companies and repertoires, theatres in Edmonton—and almost everywhere else in Canada for that matter—were not easily accessible to Canadian playwrights, though there were, as we have seen in the Maritimes and Central Canada, important exceptions. There were some exceptions in the West as well.

In Western Canada, as in the rest of the country, garrison theatricals were often staged in makeshift theatres, but permanent theatres were occasionally available to the military for their performances. Such was the case for an early Western Canadian play called *The 90th on Active Service; or, Campaigning in the North West*, described on the title page of the published edition (Winnipeg, 1885) as 'A Musical and Dramatic Burlesque in Two Acts'. Written by Staff Sergeant George Broughall during the 90th Battalion's involvement in hostilities against Louis Riel and his followers, and performed by the 90th—after the successful completion of their mission—at the Princess Opera House on 29 and 30 July 1885, *The 90th on Active Service* is a light-hearted piece in the manner of Gilbert and Sullivan, with a number of local and topical allusions. It hardly reflects the seriousness of its subject, but its joviality and jingoism were warmly appreciated by Winnipeggers, civilian and military alike. According to a review in the *Winnipeg Daily Times* (30 July 1885), a large and enthusiastic audience 'appeared to be greatly delighted with the performance, which was of a most amusing nature.' On the other hand, thought the reviewer, 'there were times when the burlesque dragged considerably, and there were many places where the pruning knife could have been applied with advantage.' The production was successful enough, however, to encourage Broughall to write another play, *The Tearful and Tragical Tale of the Tricky Troubadour; or, the Truant Tracked*, an uninspired burlesque of grand opera, published in Winnipeg in 1886 and performed at the Princess on 28 September 1886.

Another Winnipeg play was written by critic Charles Handscomb, whose views on Ibsen's *Ghosts* were quoted earlier. His comic melodrama *The Big Boom* (unpublished) was produced at the Princess on 23 November 1886. Praised by Handscomb's colleague on the *Manitoba Sun* (24 November 1886) as 'decidedly above average', *The Big Boom* commemorated the rapid economic growth of Winnipeg while 'telling of two misguided but faithful lovers and their troubles and trials'. The production starred the American actor E.A. McDowell (of *H.M.S. Parliament* fame).

Winnipeg's Princess Opera House was, then, one theatre that made a modest commitment to the staging of Canadian plays in the 1880s. It was not unique in this, but it was unusual. That there were not more, as audiences grew and theatres proliferated, can be explained in large part by audience preference for familiar and proven successes from abroad, and by the calculated exploitation of Canada by commercial theatre interests in the United States and Great Britain.

FOREIGN COMPANIES AND STARS

The history of foreign touring companies and stars in Canada is long and complex. It begins in the late eighteenth century, accelerates in the nineteenth with Canada's growing population and its improved transportation networks, reaches its peak in the last decade of the nineteenth century and the early years of the twentieth, declines rapidly prior to and following the First World War, and all but dissolves by the beginning of the Second World War. Touring gathers momentum again in the period of post-war prosperity, and productions from abroad are, of course, still seen in Canada—particularly American musicals—but such productions are now the exception rather than the rule. For almost a century of this history, British, European, and American actors and companies arranged their own tours, with the help of local contacts in Canada. Then, as the availability and the probability of large profits became apparent, business groups such as the New York Theatrical Syndicate (1896), the Shubert Theatre Corporation (1903), the British-Canadian Theatrical Organization (1912), and the Trans-Canada Theatre Society (1915) were formed to establish control over North American theatres, with the purpose of providing them with a steady supply of British and American commercially successful plays. It has been calculated that in 1908 some 313 productions toured North America out of New York, many of them visiting Canada. Influence from Great Britain was not quite so pervasive, but at its peak the Trans-Canada Theatre Society controlled 125 theatres in Canada, and major independent tours from England were still occurring in the 1930s and beyond—Sir Barry Jackson's Birmingham Repertory Theatre visit in 1931-2, for example. The cumulative effect of rising travel costs, war, the popularity of film and radio, and finally the Depression brought an end to this massive theatrical invasion from abroad. Theatrically speaking, Canada was an occupied country for most of the nineteenth century and nearly half of the twentieth. The occupation metaphor is apt, for there were pockets of limited resistance from some Canadian actors and playwrights, and there were 'collaborators', such as Ontario theatre impresario Ambrose Small. The occupation, it must be said, was not without considerable benefits. While Canadians saw a lot of mediocrity and worse, they also saw many great actors and actresses in varied and sometimes stimulating repertories. But the price was high. Although Canada built splendid theatres, and had audiences eager to fill them, Canadian playwrights, performers, and designers were given little encouragement to exercise their art in their own land. Thus when foreign professionals came no more, there remained in Canada only the outward signs of an established theatrical culture: the audiences, the theatres. For the most part, it was left to amateurs to fill the void. They did so with honour, but the country had lost a century and a half of opportunity to forge its own professional theatre identity.

Foreign theatre came in various shapes, sizes, and colours: farce, comedy, vaudeville, melodrama, occasional classics, spectacle. Spectacle could be especially profitable, and was well suited to some of the large Canadian theatres fed from New York. When C.P. Walker opened his lavish theatre in Winnipeg in 1907, for example, he was faced with the daunting task of selling close to 2,000 seats for each performance. He was not always successful, but spectacular shows like *Mazeppa* (an equestrian melodrama that brought fame to American actress Adah Isaacs Menken) and William Young's historical extravaganza *Ben Hur* could usually be relied on to fill the theatre. No commitment to Canadian talent here; Walker looked to New York for his shows. No commitment to art either; Walker's objectives were purely commercial. Action, spectacle, romance: these were saleable commodities.

C.P. Walker was an astute businessman, but the most successful, and notorious, of Canadian theatre businessmen was Ontario's Ambrose Small. Mary Brown has observed that 'between his first job as an usher in the early 1880s and his disappearance in 1919, Small changed the history of theatre in Ontario.' He changed it by creating what was close to a theatre monopoly in the province. At first in partnership with an American, C.J. Whitney, then (after Whitney's death in 1903) independently, Small acquired control of many Ontario theatres as well as others in Michigan, Ohio, and New York State. As owner, lessee, and booking agent, Small built a theatrical empire, eventually selling his interests for one and three-quarter million dollars in 1919, shortly before he disappeared without trace. (The police did not close the case, still unsolved, until 1960.)

Small was responsible for bringing an astonishing number and variety of productions from New York to his chain of theatres. Major European and American stars acted under his auspices, as did some Canadians—Julia Arthur and Margaret Anglin, for example. On the other hand Small was by no means averse to accepting groups such as the Royal Midgets, who toured in *Gulliver's Travels* in 1891, or any other dross that would sell. There was no question of diverting any profit to the development of a specifically Canadian theatrical culture, or to the promotion of theatrical art that might not necessarily be good box office. Small was interested in theatre as business, not art.

Canada's first resident foreign company seems to have been the American Company of Comedians, which performed in Halifax in the summer and fall of 1768. Another group of actors, headed by an Englishman, Edward Allen, arrived in Montreal from Albany, New York, in 1786, opening a four-month season of plays on 20 March and then moving on to Quebec City. And on Friday 25 August 1797 the circus of John B. Ricketts arrived in Montreal from New York. Other companies from the United States followed. John Bernard, an English actor who made a successful managerial career in Boston (running the Federal Street Theatre from 1806 to 1810), was in Montreal and Quebec City in 1809. The flow accelerated as the bitterness created by the War of 1812 faded, and as transportation between the United States and Canada improved—the Welland Canal was completed in 1829, and railways such as the Grand Trunk from Detroit to Montreal (1856) rapidly linked major centres—making life easier for the visiting American star. By the time Edwin Booth, brother of Lincoln's assassin, arrived in Toronto in 1876, a relatively smooth ride—in more than one sense—was assured. Despite his fame, Booth limited his appearance in Canada in 1876 to just four Ontario cities—London, Hamilton, Toronto, and St Catharines, where his performances in Shakespearean roles and as Claude Melnotte and Richelieu in Edward Bulwer-Lytton's *Lady of Lyons* and *Richelieu* were widely acclaimed.

Other notable American performers who appeared in Canada in the 1880s and 1890s were Lawrence Barrett, Mrs Fiske, James O'Neill, Robert Mantell, and many lesser lights. They were joined by numerous British actors and companies who were undeterred from plying their talents in Canada and the United States by the hazards and discomforts of nineteenth-century Atlantic crossings. All in all the experience of British actors in Canada was generally pleasurable and prosperous, and the monetary benefits were bolstered by their conviction that what they were doing was good for them and good for Canada.

One of the earliest, and certainly one of the greatest, English actors to visit Canada was Edmund Kean. The brilliance of his acting, as well as his tempestuous personal life, brought him fame and notoriety on both sides of the Atlantic. Kean opened his Canadian engagement in Montreal on 31 July 1826 as Richard III, repeating the role on 4 September 1826 when he moved to Quebec City, where he stayed for a month. Although his final appearance in Quebec City was marred by a mini-riot (for which Kean bore no responsibility), the English actor's sojourn in Canada was a great triumph and paved the way for many other British successes. Indeed, such was the demand for British theatrical fare in nineteenth- and early-twentieth-century Canada, that few companies lost money. The trick was to keep risk to a minimum by providing what audiences expected to get—productions for which actors had become famous in London. Among these famous British actors were Fanny Kemble, Charles Kean (Edmund's son), and Ellen Kean (Charles's wife), and Sir Henry Irving—the first actor to be knighted. Irving was a master at extracting the highest possible profit from tours of Canada and the United States; from his eight visits Irving made a profit of well over half a million dollars from total receipts of three and a half million.

Another prominent actress who visited Canada was the eccentric and temperamental Mrs Patrick Campbell. Remembered for creating major roles such as Paula Tanqueray in Arthur Wing Pinero's *The Second Mrs Tanqueray* (1893) and Eliza Doolittle in Shaw's *Pygmalion* (1914), as well as for her stormy relationship with Shaw, Mrs Campbell made a number of visits to North America. On a bitterly cold night early in 1908 she began an engagement in *The Second Mrs Tanqueray* at Winnipeg's Walker Theatre, but not before she had smashed several windows because she found the theatre too hot, and had threatened to cancel the performance because she was upset, for some reason, with her New York managers. John Martin-Harvey first visited Canada as an insignificant member of Henry Irving's Lyceum Company in 1884. His impressions of that occasion are not recorded, but he devotes two full chapters of his autobiography to the tours he later undertook with his own company. He crossed Canada fourteen times, becoming so accustomed to the journey that he thought 'no more of our six or seven thousand miles' travelling than as of a pleasant winter pilgrimage, and of the Atlantic no more than as of a ferry.' Martin-Harvey presented mostly popular melodrama and an occasional Shakespeare play. Some innovative moments, however, included a remarkable episode in Calgary when Martin-Harvey invited the chief and leaders of the Sarcee Indian tribe to attend a performance of *Oedipus Rex*. The Indians occupied the boxes and maintained a worrying inscrutability throughout the play; but they must have been impressed, for they duly honoured Martin-Harvey by making him an honorary chief—just as Edmund Kean had been honoured by Huron Indians a century before.

Despite language difficulties, and the problems of coping with alien North American customs and conventions, European stars, like their British counterparts, were also strongly attracted by the opportunities of commercial success in North America.

Among the several European actors to visit Canada was the great Italian actor Tommaso Salvini. There were many remarkable things about Salvini's performance as Othello at Toronto's Grand Opera House on 21 February 1881, not least that he delivered his lines in Italian, while the rest of the company acted in English. Such an occurrence was not uncommon with the many European actors who toured North America. Ernesto Rossi, Salvini's contemporary, exploited his lack of English on an 1881–2 tour of America by gradually introducing lines of English into his performances, startling an audience in Charleston in December 1881 by suddenly breaking into English with Lear's 'Every inch a king' and then reverting to Italian. By the time he did Lear again in New York in January 1882, he managed the whole final act in English.

CANADIAN COMPANIES AND STARS

Despite the growing dominance of foreign companies and performers, it was still possible to establish a professional theatre career in Canada in the nineteenth century. Charlotte Morrison, for example, born in Quebec in 1832, managed a stock company at Toronto's Grand Opera House in the 1870s, with thirty-week repertory seasons ranging from Shakespeare to farce. Admittedly, the company regularly hosted visiting American stars, but the experience and training provided by Mrs Morrison was solid enough to prepare at least one member of the company for an independent managerial career. After leaving the Grand to act in the Maritimes, Ida van Cortland—in partnership with her husband, Albert Tavernier, an actor whom she married in 1880—formed a company that toured extensively in Canada, as far west as Winnipeg and as far east as St John's, but principally in Ontario, until disbanding in 1896. Because the Tavernier Dramatic Company did not have the resources to compete with the large American touring companies, which came to monopolize Canada's major theatres, they concentrated on the smaller towns generally ignored by New York, with a repertoire of popular melodrama and comedy. This formula was also followed, with great success, by the Marks Brothers, another company that originated and remained in Canada, with some forays into the United States—a pleasing reversal of the normal process.

The various companies of the Marks Brothers (five brothers, with wives and children involved as well) toured Canada regularly from 1879 to 1922. They survived for so long because they understood the values and tastes of Canadian small-town audiences. As Robert Marks explained: 'The great appetite of the masses of showgoers today is for melodrama. Despite what "experts" say, melodrama [such as *Uncle Tom's Cabin* and *East Lynne*] is the one great perennial in the theatrical business. We have been playing melodrama for over thirty years, and they never fail to draw, except in the bigger towns where the public is made over-fastidious by frequent visits of the two-dollar companies. And of all shows the clean show is the winner. For the lifetime of the Marks enterprises our people have absolutely refused to compromise on honest and orderly entertainment' (*Billboard*, 19 November 1921). Robert Marks' philosophy of entertainment was shared by Canadian actor-manager H. Price Webber, whose company toured melodramas throughout the Maritimes, Quebec, and New England until 1915.

Other actors and managers who made a successful living from theatre in Canada in the nineteenth century included John Nickinson (Charlotte Morrison's father), a British soldier who acted in garrison theatricals in Quebec City and Montreal and stayed in Canada to run Toronto's Royal Lyceum Theatre from 1853 to 1859, and Harold Nelson—singer, actor, and elocution teacher—born and educated in the Maritimes, who took serious drama to many Western Canadian cities, nurturing acting talent as he did so. As the population of Canada grew, and as more theatres were built, the opportunities for professionals like the Taverniers and Nelson increased. By 1898 the *Canadian Magazine* could claim that 'the number of Canadians winning fame at home and abroad justifies "The Canadian" in devoting some attention to the stage.' There followed a series of articles by W.J. Thorold, himself an actor. A decade later, an article, 'Successful Canadian Players', in *Canadian West Monthly* (July 1909) discussed some fifty Canadian actors, actresses, and singers.

That so many Canadians made their mark on the stage in the late nineteenth century is a notable achievement; but for many of them success was measured, as it is today, by the degree of foreign, not Canadian, acclaim they won. That is, their sights were set on American (and, to a lesser extent, British) theatres, audiences, critics, and impresarios. The reasons for working in the United States were colonial as much as they were economic, based on an assumption that standards in New York or Boston were higher than those in Toronto or Edmonton or Montreal. In the nineteenth century this assumption went unchallenged, and thus no strong body of professional acting talent was based in Canada until after the founding of the Stratford Festival in 1953. McKee Rankin offers an interesting case in point. Born in Sandwich, Ontario, in 1841, Rankin acted periodically in Canada, but he began his career in Rochester, N.Y., and it was in the United States that he sought to make his reputation. First with his wife, Kitty Blanchard, and later with Nance O'Neill, Rankin starred throughout the United States, and in England, in a number of common-or-garden melodramas, such as Joaquin Miller's *The Danites*, and *The Two Orphans* (adapted by Hart Jackson from D'Ennery and Cormon's French original, *Les Deux orphelines*). Rankin's Macbeth also attracted some attention, but he was better remembered for his more typical efforts in roles such as Jacques Frochard in *The Two Orphans*. He died on 17 April 1914.

Like Rankin, Julia Arthur was born in Ontario (in Hamilton, 3 May 1869) and was quick to ally herself with an American company. After some childhood experience in Hamilton, she successfully auditioned for Daniel Bandmann and joined his Shakespeare Repertory Company when she was only fourteen. Julia Arthur acted with other American touring and stock companies before going to London, England, where she was taken on by Henry Irving's Lyceum Company in 1895. At the Lyceum she was in competition with Ellen Terry, and it seems she did not always behave as deferentially as was perhaps expected of a young lady from Canada. At any rate, she left in 1897, having become, according to Laurence Irving, 'a little temperamental—a luxury in which, at the Lyceum, only Ellen Terry was allowed to indulge.' Returning to the United States, Julia Arthur founded her own touring company, and, in 1898, married B.P. Cheney, a wealthy Boston businessman. She retired from the stage in 1924 (after touring Canada in *Saint Joan*), by which time she had played the female lead in some two hundred plays, including Lady Windermere in the first North American production of Wilde's play.

Margaret Anglin (born in Ottawa, 3 April 1876) was another Canadian actress who welcomed the challenges of Shakespeare and Shaw. Writing of her performance in Sardou's *Diplomacy* at New York's Empire Theatre in April 1901, one reviewer, according to sources cited by William C. Young, claimed that 'Miss Anglin could wring emotion from a keg of nails . . . one had to wink considerably to dodge the moisture engendered by her Dora.' But she also excelled in Shakespeare (especially as Viola and Ophelia) and as Shaw's Joan. Margaret Anglin's most distinctive contribution to the theatre lay, however, in her stagings of Greek plays in the Hearst Greek theatre at the University of California, Berkeley, where between 1910 and 1927 she produced and acted in the *Antigone* and *Electra* of Sophocles, and the *Iphigenia in Aulis*, *Medea*, and *Hippolytus* of Euripides.

Like Julia Arthur, Franklin McLeay from Watford, Ontario, was prominent in England. He was a talented actor with Wilson Barrett's company at His Majesty's Theatre in London, where he triumphed as Cassius. He died from pneumonia, three days after organizing and appearing in a benefit performance of *Othello* for families left homeless by the 1900 Ottawa fire. According to critic Hector Charlesworth, many London actors believed that McLeay 'would have become known as the greatest actor of the twentieth century'.

McLeay, Anglin, Arthur, Rankin, and other Canadian actors (Marie Dressler and Henry Miller for example) were intent on achieving success in American and British theatres. Some of their colleagues— Harold Nelson, the Taverniers, the Marks Brothers among them— stayed at home to practise their profession. Meanwhile, American and British interests tightened their control of Canadian theatres and continued to promote their own plays and playwrights. In the circumstances, it is not surprising that by the outbreak of the First World War Canada had not succeeded in creating its own theatrical identity. For some Canadians there was nothing alarming or surprising about this. As Canadian playwright J.E. Middleton wrote in 1914, 'Canada has always been indebted either directly or indirectly to the United States for her drama. Even the English plays and players go to the Dominion today by way of New York. Nor is this a cause for complaint. It is a natural condition.' Natural it might have been, but for a number of Canadians in the early years of the twentieth century it was an increasingly unsatisfactory condition. As Canada's involvement and military achievements in the First World War generated greater national awareness, and as the country's painters (the Group of Seven was formed in 1920) set artistic examples, more and more voices were raised against foreign domination of Canadian theatre, and ideas began to proliferate about a national theatrical identity—what it meant for Canada, and how it could be achieved.

BERNARD, JOHN. *Retrospections of America, 1797–1811*, ed. Laurence Hutton and Brander Matthews. New York, Harper, 1887.

BERNHARDT, SARAH. *My Double Life. Memoirs of Sarah Bernhardt*. London, Heinemann, 1907.

BOOTH, MICHAEL. 'Gold Rush Theatres of the Klondike.' *Beaver*, 292 (1962), 32–7.

BROWN, MARY. 'Ambrose Small: A Ghost in Spite of Himself.' *Theatrical Touring and Founding in North America*, ed. L.W. Conolly. Westport, Greenwood Press, 1982.

CHARLESWORTH, HECTOR. *Candid Chronicles*. Toronto, Macmillan, 1925.

——. *More Candid Chronicles*. Toronto, Macmillan, 1928.

COWELL, MR & MRS S. *The Cowells in America. Being the Diary of Mrs. Sam Cowell during Her Husband's Concert Tour in the Years 1860–1861*, ed. M. Willson Disher. London, Oxford University Press, 1934.

DE FONTAINE, F.G., ed. *Birds of a Feather; or, Talks with Sothern*. New York, G.W. Carleton, 1878.

DYOTT, WILLIAM. *Dyott's Diary 1781–1845. A Selection from the Journal of William Dyott, Sometime General in the British Army and Aide-de-Camp to His Majesty King George III*, ed. Reginald W. Jeffrey. London, Constable, 1907.

EDWARDS, MURRAY. *A Stage in Our Past. English-Language Theatre in Eastern Canada from the 1790s to 1914*. Toronto, University of Toronto Press, 1968.

ELIOT, WILLIAM. *Naval Sketch-Book, or Service Afloat and Ashore*. London, Henry Colburn, 1826.

FIRTH, EDITH B. *The Town of York, 1793–1815*. Toronto, Champlain Society, 1962. [For Maria Jarvis' account of the 1809 Toronto production of *The School for Scandal*.]

FRYE, NORTHROP. *The Bush Garden. Essays on the Canadian Imagination*. Toronto, Anansi Press, 1971.

GRAHAM, FRANKLIN. *Histrionic Montreal. Annals of the Montreal Stage with Biographical and Critical Notices of the Plays and Players of a Century*. Montreal, Lovell, 1902.

HAKLUYT, RICHARD. *Richard Hakluyt: Voyages and Documents*, ed. Janet Hampden. London, Oxford University Press, 1958. [For the 1583 expedition of Sir Humphrey Gilbert.]

HAM, GEORGE H. *Reminiscences of a Raconteur between the '40s and the '20s*. Toronto, Musson Book Co., 1921.

HARVEY, RUTH. *Curtain Time*. Boston and Cambridge, Houghton Mifflin, 1949.

HERRING, FRANCES E. *In the Pathless West, with Soldiers, Pioneers, Miners, and Savages*. London, T.F. Unwin, 1904.

HOFFMAN, JAMES. 'Towards an Early British Columbia Theatre: The Hamatsa Ceremony as Drama.' *Canadian Drama, L'Art dramatique canadien*, 11 (1985), 231–44.

IRVING, LAURENCE. *Henry Irving: The Actor and His World*. London, Faber & Faber, 1951.

KLINCK, CARL F. *Wilfred Campbell. A Study in Late Provincial Victorianism*. Toronto, Ryerson Press, 1942.

LAMBERT, JOHN. *Travels through Lower Canada and the United States of North America in the Years 1806, 1807, and 1808*. London, Richard Phillips, 1810.

MARTIN-HARVEY, JOHN. *The Autobiography of Sir John Martin-Harvey*. London, Sampson, Low, Marston, [1933].

MAYER, DAVID. 'Towards a Definition of Popular Theatre.' *Western Popular Theatre*, ed. David Mayer and Kenneth Richards. London, Methuen, 1977.

MIDDLETON, J.E. 'The Theatre in Canada.' *Canada and its Provinces*, ed. Adam Shortt and Arthur G. Doughty. Volume 12. Toronto, Glasgow, Brook & Co., 1914.

O'NEILL, PATRICK. 'A Checklist of Canadian Dramatic Materials.' *Canadian Drama, L'Art dramatique canadien*, 8 (1982), 176-303 and 9 (1983), 369–506.

SHRIVE, NORMAN. 'Poets and Patriotism.' *Canadian Literature*, 20 (1964), 15–26. [On Charles Mair.]

TAIT, MICHAEL. 'Playwrights in a Vacuum: English-Canadian Drama in the Nineteenth-Century.' *Canadian Literature*, 16 (1963), 5–18.

WAGNER, ANTON, ed. *Canada's Lost Plays*. Toronto, CTR Publications. Volume 1: *The Nineteenth Century* (1978); Volume 2: *Women Pioneers* (1979); Volume 3: *The Developing Mosaic* (1980); Volume 4: *Colonial Quebec; French-Canadian Drama 1606-1966* (1982).

——, ed. *The Brock Bibliography of Published Canadian Plays in English 1766-1978*. Toronto, Playwrights Press, 1980.

YOUNG, WILLIAM C. *Famous Actors and Actresses on the American Stage*. New York, Bowker, 1975.

Dominion Drama Festival poster, 1933. Courtesy Mrs Betty Boylen Sumner.

2

TOWARDS A CANADIAN
THEATRICAL IDENTITY

THE LITTLE THEATRE MOVEMENT

Critic B. K. Sandwell was a forceful opponent of American domination of Canadian theatre. In an article published in the *Canadian Magazine* in November 1911 he voiced a strong protest against what he called the 'annexation' of the Canadian stage by the American syndicates. As far as the syndicates were concerned, Sandwell argued, 'Ontario is as much tributary to the offices on either side of Broadway as is Minnesota, and . . . British Columbia is parcelled out like New Jersey.'

> . . . Canada is the only nation in the world whose stage is entirely controlled by aliens. She is the only nation in the world whose sons and daughters are compelled to go to a foreign capital for permission to act in their own language on the boards of their own theatres. The only road to the applause of a Toronto theatre audience is by way of Broadway. The Montreal girl who wants to show her own people that she can act must sign an agreement with a New York manager . . .

For Sandwell, however, the answer to the problem of American domination was not an independent Canadian theatre, but closer links to Britain—more British touring companies, with more British plays. John Martin-Harvey postulated in the *University Magazine* in April 1914 a close link between the 'national Canadian character' and 'the fostering of imperial ideas', and in 1928 the English actress Ellaline Terriss spoke firmly about the imperial function of British drama in Canada: 'It was here [Toronto] more than at any other city we visited that we heard on all sides the demand for British attractions.

Rightly so, the people of this great metropolis feel that there can be no greater link of Empire than the continual arrival of British artists to show young Canada not only our modern plays, but also the English classics, which are, of course, as much their property as they are ours.' For another British writer, Harold Terry, writing in *Outlook* (7 February 1914), American plays were a 'menace to Imperial progress', one 'recognized fully by thinking men and women throughout the Dominion.' According to Terry the solution lay in a stronger British theatrical presence in Canada—but he also recognized that at some point 'the Dominion will possess its own drama and will need no longer to rely entirely upon the Mother-country and the States for its supplies.'

The process towards theatrical independence was, ironically, accelerated by the rise of alternative forms of entertainment in Canada—film and radio—which caused theatre attendance to decrease, making tours by American and British companies financially hazardous. The vacuum left by the decline of the touring companies was filled for some time by several professional stock companies. The Rex Stock Company, for example, presented seasons in several Ontario towns and cities in the early 1920s, as did the Mae Edwards Players. Born in Lindsay, Ontario, in 1878, Mae Edwards took her company to communities throughout Ontario and the Maritimes—as well as into the United States—until as late as 1935. In Ottawa the Galvin Players occupied the Capitol Theatre for nearly three years (1927–9), though the parent company—the Galvin Producing Company—was American. Theatre historian Ross Stuart has suggested that Western Canada was 'overflowing with stock companies'. Some were extremely successful. The Winnipeg-based Permanent Players ran for twenty-one consecutive seasons in the Winnipeg Theatre. The Ray Brandon Players of Kamloops, on the other hand, went bankrupt in fairly short order, but not before future film star Boris Karloff had established a niche with the company as the resident villain. Other stock companies identified by Stuart as prominent in the West in the early years of this century include the Dominion Stock Company, the Eckhardt Players, the Empress Company, and the Allen Players.

These stock companies provide ample evidence of the viability of a professional Canadian theatre largely independent of direct British or American control. Nonetheless, the repertoires of the stock companies—consisting as they did of Broadway and West End successes, popular light comedies, melodramas, and vaudeville—remained highly derivative, and production values were necessarily dictated by profit margins rather than artistic considerations.

The inspiration for the development of a genuinely Canadian theatre came from the art theatres of Europe—such as J.T. Grein's Independent Theatre Club in London (formed in 1891), or the Abbey Theatre in Dublin (1904). Eschewing commercial ideology and expectations, the Little Theatre movement dedicated itself to innovation and experiment in dramatic production, frequently giving priority to new Canadian plays. In outlook, in method, and in values, the Little Theatres of Canada differed from commercial theatre—whether Canadian stock or foreign touring—as Hyperion to a satyr.

A seminal organization in the development of new principles and objectives for Canadian theatre was the Arts and Letters Players of Toronto. These actors, directors, artists, and writers (including Roy Mitchell, Arthur Lismer, and Lawren Harris) were members of the Arts and Letters Club, founded in 1908, the year the Players began life in a small room in the Old Court House on Adelaide Street. The group's 'adamantine rule' for the production of plays—as Merrill Denison explained in a tribute to the Arts and Letters Players in the *Canadian Bookman* in February 1923—was 'never to produce anything that had been done in Canada before'. They performed a repertoire of Maeterlinck, Yeats, Synge, Tagore, Lady Gregory, and other contemporary playwrights in a room without a stage, little or no scenery, and lighting equipment made of tin wash-basins, biscuit boxes, and stove pipes. Plans for a new facility were interrupted by the First World War, but in 1919 the opening of Hart House Theatre at the University of Toronto fulfilled this obvious need.

Roy Mitchell had been the driving force behind the Arts and Letter Players and his involvement with amateur theatre continued in his role as first director of Hart House Theatre (1919–21). An American by birth, Mitchell spent most of his career as a teacher and director in the United States, but his innovative ideas about theatre (expressed in his influential 1929 book, *Creative Theatre*) took root in Toronto. Rejecting what he perceived as the moral and aesthetic bankruptcy of commercial theatre, Mitchell set about making Hart House Theatre a place to nurture and challenge Canadian directors, designers, actors, technicians, playwrights, and audiences. The theatre itself—unlike what Mitchell had coped with at the Court House—was first-rate. Built as an afterthought in the basement of Hart House, it seated some 500 people in a comfortable auditorium. It was technically advanced and well staffed, as a description in the December 1920 issue of *Canadian Bookman* testifies:

> In addition to its superb mechanism, with the third largest stage switch-board in America, a mile and half of electric conduit, capacity up to 80,000 watts of electrical illumination, a rotary cyclorama, upwards of 70 lamp houses of all styles, special effects for smoke, flame, moonlight ripple, flowing water, rain, cloud and lightning, complete workshops, paint studios, wardrobes with power machines and dyeing apparatus, papier maché plant and plaster cast equipment, the theatre carries a professional staff of eight persons, and a number of apprentices and paid casual workers. It has a professional director, his assistant, a musical director, a directress of wardrobes, a directress of property shop, a carpenter, a head cleaner and treasurer, who supervise and perform most of the work connected with the making of a production.

Like the Arts and Letters Players, Hart House presented a repertoire of contemporary drama (with lots of Shaw) and the classics, but also regularly performed Canadian plays. Although the theatre no longer occupies the prominent place it once did, it was one of the leaders in the reaction against theatrical commercialism. The careers of many distinguished actors and directors were fostered at Hart House: Jane Mallet, Dora Mavor Moore, Andrew Allan, Donald and Murray Davis, Robert Gill, William Hutt, Donald Sutherland, Charmion King, and Kate Reid, for example.

Among the playwrights who responded to Roy Mitchell's leadership at Hart House was Merrill Denison. Like Mitchell, Denison was born in the United States (of a Canadian mother and American father), but throughout the 1920s he was at the forefront of Canada's Little Theatre movement, eventually producing a body of dramatic work superior to any previously written in English Canada. Denison's *The Unheroic North: Four Canadian Plays* (1923) contains three short plays—*Brothers in Arms* (first produced at Hart House Theatre on 5 April 1921), *The Weather Breeder* (Hart House, 21 April 1924), *From Their Own Place* (Arts and Letters Players, 25 April 1922)—and the full-length *Marsh Hay*, not produced until March 1974, again at Hart House. Set in the backwoods of northern Ontario, the short plays are amusing satires on the eccentricities and mores of back-woods people, astutely capturing their environment and turn of speech. *Marsh Hay*, on the other hand, is a powerful and harrowing portrayal of the tragic futility of these people's lives and the brutalizing effect of poverty upon them. In its bleakness and uncompromising view of human relations, *Marsh Hay* bears comparison with John Millington Synge's *Well of the Saints*. John Serang, feeling trapped by marriage and by twenty years 'workin fifty acres of grey stone and cuttin marsh hay', explodes cruelly against his wife and her childbearing: 'A good wife? Do you call havin another young one every year . . . bein a good wife? Bringin along another mouth to feed, year by year, on fifty acres of grey stone? Twelve! Do you call that bein a good wife? Wife? More like a damned sow.' Their promiscuous sixteen-year-old daughter, Sarilin, becomes pregnant, deliberately miscarries, but on recovery starts another sexual affair. At the play's close, in a passage almost identical to that ending Act 1, she goes to another assignation, to begin (probably) another squalid cycle of pregnancy and abortion.

> *The man*: (*In an intense whisper*) What kept you?
> *Sarilin*: Sh! Maw and paw sent me to bed.
> *The man*: I been waitin an hour. Come on!
> *Sarilin*: All right.
> (*He takes her arms roughly and just before they go swings her to him and kisses her viciously, her head bent far back.*)

While there is uncertain psychology in the character of the mother—especially in her attitude to the pregnant Sarilin—*Marsh Hay* is distinguished by an uncommon honesty of vision, authenticity of speech, and a command of dramatic structure. The themes of entrap-ment by family ties, poverty, and bondage to a hostile land are commonplace in Canadian literature between the wars and may be seen in novels like Sinclair Ross's *As For Me and My House* (1941), in the political protest plays of the 1930s, and in Gwen Pharis Ringwood's *Still Stands the House* (1939).

Denison also made a significant contribution to radio drama (then in its infancy). His *Henry Hudson and Other Plays* (1931) dramatizes important events and figures in Canadian history. These six plays

(*Henry Hudson*, *Pierre Radisson*, *Montcalm*, *Seven Oaks*, *Laura Secord*, *Alexander Mackenzie*), directed by Tyrone Guthrie on his first visit to Canada for broadcast on CNRM, Montreal, in 1931–2, represent a serious and skilful attempt to rescue Canada's past and exploit Canadian sources in a historical series. Denison shows a surprisingly mature grasp of the new medium, and his treatment of his subjects is fresh and unsentimental. In *Laura Secord*, for example, he makes no attempt to glamorize Laura Secord's heroism, and his treatment of both Montcalm and Wolfe in *Montcalm* is even-handed, encapsulating a remarkable amount of historical detail within a dramatic format that transcends the mere documentary.

Two more Denison one-act plays, *Balm* and *The Prizewinner*, were first produced at Hart House Theatre (in August 1923 and February 1928, respectively), the former being published in one of the most significant collections of Canadian plays to appear between the wars, *Canadian Plays from Hart House*. Edited by Vincent Massey, and published in two volumes (1926, 1927), the collection contains eleven plays, eight one-acts in volume one and three full-length in volume two. Merrill Denison is represented by three plays in the first volume (*Balm*, *Brothers in Arms*, and *The Weather Breeder*), and there are also plays by Duncan Campbell Scott (*Pierre*, a domestic melodrama set in a Quebec village), Marian Osborne (*The Point of View*, an amusing domestic comedy owing something to Shaw's *Heartbreak House*), Henry Borsook (*Three Weddings of a Hunchback*, a black comedy), Isabel MacKay (*The Second Lie*, a psychological drama), and Britton Cooke (*The Translation of John Snaith*, a melodrama). Of the three plays in the second volume, two are unremarkable—Louis Alexander MacKay's *The Freedom of Jean Guichet* is a domestic tragi-comedy in which a husband rebels against his domineering wife, and Leslie Reid's *Trespassers* is a toothless comedy about a chauvinistic English Member of Parliament. The third play, however—Carroll Aikins' *The God of Gods*—is a notable portrayal of Indian manners and mores that, while lacking the toughness of George Ryga's dramas of Indian life, nonetheless presents a refreshingly unsentimental story of two Indian lovers. *The God of Gods* also had the distinction of receiving its première (in November 1919) at the Birmingham Repertory Theatre, then one of the leading art theatres in England. Carroll Aikins went on to form his own theatre, the Home Theatre, near Naramata, British Columbia. It survived for only two seasons (1920–2), but Aikins later became director of Hart House Theatre (1927–9).

Hart House Theatre was the most prominent of Canada's Little Theatres, but many others were established across the country, including the Ottawa Drama League (1913), the Vancouver Little Theatre (1921), the Community Players of Winnipeg (1921), the Montreal Repertory Theatre (1930), and the Halifax Theatre Arts Guild (1931). All shared a desire to create a Canadian theatre, but perhaps the best example of a commitment to Canadian creativity is Herman Voaden's work with the Sarnia Little Theatre, founded in 1927.

Voaden was one of the most inventive contributors to twentieth-century Canadian theatre. His reach exceeded his grasp, but his innovative, and in some cases unrealistic, ideas challenged conventional thinking. He studied theatre (at the Yale School of Drama, 1930–1, and on a number of visits to Germany between 1928 and 1933); he theorized about it (in essays, interviews, and in his introduction to *Six Canadian Plays*, published in 1930, and in other books); he taught it (at Toronto's Central High School of Commerce, Queen's University, and the University of Toronto); he administered it (as President of the Canadian Arts Council and as National Director of the Canadian Conference of the Arts); and, above all, he practised it, most notably as a playwright and director.

At Sarnia Voaden's zeal and inspiration were evident from the beginning. His work there came to symbolize the artistic and nationalistic objectives of the Canadian Little Theatre movement, the desire for 'the development of a national consciousness and a national culture', as critic Lawrence Mason put it in the Toronto *Globe* on 3 November 1928. Voaden produced Shaw, Yeats, Denison and other contemporary playwrights at Sarnia but it is his own plays, together with his theory of drama, that call for particular attention.

In Germany Voaden had fallen under the influence of German Expressionist drama, especially that of Georg Kaiser and Ernst Toller. Key features of this drama include the *Stationentechnik* (a dramatic technique presenting the various states of the protagonist's development), *Wandlung* (the regeneration and transfiguration of the protagonist), and the use of types (Man, Woman, Waiter) rather than individual characters. Utilizing its fluidity (multiple playing areas were created by spot lighting and easily identifiable props), Voaden developed his own theory of drama, a coalescence of many diverse art forms into a composite theatrical unity that he called 'Symphonic Expressionism'. He described his theory in an article in the *Globe*, 17 December 1932, concluding it with a strong appeal:

> Let us bring to the theatre the solidity and power of sculpture and architecture, the glory of painting, the spiritual immediacy of music. Let us restore to it the greatness of poetry, dance and ritual it once knew. Let us continue then in new plays written and produced in a language richer and more complete than heretofore evolved.

Voaden put his theory into practice by attempting to dramatize a vision of a mythic and heroic Canadian North (as opposed to Denison's 'unheroic North'): the North tests people's courage, and if they endure they experience rebirth and regeneration. The 1930 *Symphony: A Drama of Motion and Light For A New Theatre* (written with Lowrie Warrener) exemplifies at once the power of Voaden's vision and the inadequacy of his theatrical conventions to express it. The plot of *Symphony* is simple and archetypal: the protagonist, Man, flees the city and its destructiveness for the Northern wilderness where he achieves 'a new strength and courage'. He marries, has a child, the Woman dies. Man's pilgrimage now brings him to the prairies where drought and hail destroy his crops. Finally, alone on a mountain, he experiences a spiritual transfiguration. Lacking dialogue, however, *Symphony* is hardly a play at all; it is, perhaps, a scenario for a ballet.

Subsequent Voaden plays include *Rocks* (produced in Toronto in April 1932), *Earth Song* (produced in Sarnia in December 1932), *Hill-Land* (produced in Toronto in December 1934), and *Murder Pattern* (produced in Toronto in January 1936). All four are flawed by a narrative structure that detracts from their dramatic impetus. B.K. Sandwell, reviewing *Hill-Land* in *Saturday Night* (22 December 1934), noted this: 'One of Mr. Voaden's claims for his "newer theatre" is that it "will have the novel's capacity for reflective comment and varied interpretation". . . . What has restricted reflective comment in the theatre is not the absence of electric light but the fact that it is a *performance*, not a narrative. . . .' No amount of music, dance, scenery, and special effects can compensate for the absence of dramatic tension and psychological depth in the play. Paradoxically, *Murder Pattern*, which is furthest removed (though not divorced) from his Expressionist theories, is Voaden's best work. Despite its uneasy marriage of Realism and Expressionism, the play builds to an impressive intensity where, in the final threnody, the murderer is seen to have been purged of his crime (based on an actual Ontario case) by his mystical union with the cleansing forms of Nature.

Notwithstanding the admirable energy of Voaden's ideas and theatrical innovation, his influence was slight; his theatrical experimentation is primarily a matter of historical interest.

The Little Theatre movement in Canada, as in the United States and Europe, began with a sense of mission—essentially to create theatrical art rather than to passively receive or duplicate the commercial enterprises of other nations. In the 1930s that sense of mission began to fade, as the Little Theatre movement sought to become socially acceptable and (within the modest bounds of amateur theatre) commercially successful. Rupert Caplan had written a short article for the October 1928 issue of *Canadian Forum* in which he extolled the principles and objectives of the country's Little Theatres, but in November 1939 *Curtain Call*, Canada's first English-language theatre magazine, published what amounted to an obituary for these same principles and objectives: 'A cause . . . injects red life-blood into an organization and unless the Little Theatre regains the fervour of its cause, it will have none of that life-blood; it will become anaemic. It may last as a living corpse for some time but it will be swept away by organizations vital with life because they have a mission, aims, and ideals.' The writer of this article, Lockie Campbell, concluded that the Little Theatres of Canada were close to being a 'lost cause'. They were not—and are not—but after the heady days of the Arts and Letters Players and Hart House Theatre a new initiative was needed.

THE DOMINION DRAMA FESTIVAL

Voaden and other critics argued in the 1920s and 1930s for some kind of centralized administrative structure to co-ordinate the activities of Canada's many Little Theatres in an attempt to give them a sense of national identity and purpose. The Dominion Drama Festival was such a structure. Preceded by the Earl Grey Musical and Dramatic

Competitions (1907–11) and succeeded by Theatre Canada, the DDF was in a very real sense, for more than thirty years (1932–70)—with a hiatus during the war years—Canada's national theatre. (CBC Radio drama also has a claim to that title.) The Festival provided incentives and opportunities for actors, directors, playwrights, designers, and technicians; it built and maintained audiences across the country; it kept theatre in the public eye; ultimately it created the circumstances that made Canadian professional theatre possible in the 1950s. As Robertson Davies has pointed out (in his foreword to Betty Lee's *Love and Whisky: The Story of the Dominion Drama Festival*, 1973), 'the foundation of our modern professional theatre rests on many stones, but the largest and strongest is the achievement of the Dominion Drama Festival. The professionals may forget that, and it will do no harm if they do so, but the historians of art must never forget.' Run by amateurs, the DDF sometimes behaved amateurishly; its officials sometimes bungled; like any organization it had its rows and dissensions; it could be silly, it could be dull. But it had successes as well as failures. The small groups of enthusiasts, led by the Governor General, the Earl of Bessborough, who met in Ottawa on Saturday 29 October 1932 to form the DDF, set in motion an institution whose contribution to Canadian theatre was unprecedented.

The various committees of the DDF quickly came up with a set of rules to govern the first Festival, held in Ottawa in April 1933. The rules were frequently changed; the basic system, however, involved holding a series of regional festivals (all seen and judged by a single travelling adjudicator, usually from France or England), and then, on the basis of the regional adjudicator's recommendations, issuing invitations to groups to participate in a week-long final competition held in a major city, where prizes were awarded in a number of production categories. Again, one adjudicator (different from the regional adjudicator but also usually from abroad) saw all the plays and gave public assessments before handing out the prizes.

A significant limitation of the DDF was that its energy was directed only partially to matters theatrical. White ties and tails were *de rigueur* on opening and closing nights of the Festival, and playwright John Coulter recalls that the Festival 'spawned from Christmas until early summer a continuous round of parties with no stint on drinks, with the ladies, at least during competition weeks, dressed to the fairest of

Vanity Fair, and the men—I had never before seen so many black ties and white ties inspecting each other in one place.' Betty Lee calls a chapter of her history of the DDF 'The Social Side', providing ample evidence of the emphasis on protocol, receptions, balls, and dinner parties, and aptly quoting Tom Hendry's remark, 'Why, I once heard one of the governors remark that the DDF could be a really nice organization if only it didn't have to put on those damned plays.'

Yet despite the Festival's conservatism, erratic standards, and social élitism, its achievements were considerable. In providing opportunities for actors and directors such as Frances Hyland, William Hutt, Martha Allan, John Colicos, Kate Reid, Amelia Hall, Douglas Rain, William Needles, and many others, it helped train the leading professionals of today's theatre, and although the bulk of Canadian plays written for performance at DDF competitions is scarcely memorable, some major playwrights emerged under its auspices.

John Coulter, for example, after moving to Canada from Ireland and England in 1936, presented his one-act comedy *The House in the Quiet Glen* at the 1937 Festival, where it won the best-play award. Originally produced on BBC radio in 1925 as *Sally's Choice*, directed by Tyrone Guthrie, *The House in the Quiet Glen* is an amusing if somewhat predictable work about a young Irish woman's dilemma when her parents choose as her bridegroom the widowed father of the man she really wants to marry. Another DDF success for Coulter was a more serious play, *The Drums Are Out*, which won the best-Canadian-play award at the 1950 Festival in Toronto. Set in Belfast during the turbulence of the 1920s, it premièred at Dublin's Abbey Theatre in 1948. The play explores the tensions in a Protestant family when a daughter secretly marries an IRA leader. Though successfully achieving some degree of dramatic tension, *The Drums Are Out* pales in comparison to Sean O'Casey's plays on similar themes.

Coulter wrote other plays on Irish subjects, some of which had significant Canadian productions—*The Family Portrait* at Hart House in 1938, *Holy Manhattan* at the Arts and Letters Club in 1940, and several on CBC radio and television. It is for his three plays on a Canadian subject—Louis Riel—however, that Coulter is best remembered. The first and most ambitious of the three is *Riel*, first produced by Toronto's New Play Society in February 1950, starring Mavor Moore as Riel, and directed by Don Harron. A play of epic proportions, with some thirty scenes and a very large cast, *Riel* documents the events of the 1869–70 and 1885 Métis rebellions, culminating in the trial and execution of Riel. There are moments of gripping tension—the brief struggle between Riel and the Fenian W.B. O'Donoghue over the flying of the Union Jack before hostilities break out in Part One; the scenes of anti-and pro-Riel mobs driven by religious fanaticism; parts of the trial. But ultimately the play must be judged a failure. It is in the trial scene—where the tension should be at its highest, even if (as in Shaw's *Saint Joan*) we know the outcome—that the fundamental weakness of *Riel* is apparent. Speaking in his own defence, Riel is polite and reasonable to a fault; Coulter gives him a damp squib of a speech. What is missing from the whole play, in fact, is a strong point of view. Riel is a controversial character; Coulter shows us a wide spectrum of his emotions and thoughts but leads us to no particular conclusion. There are contentious political and religious issues in *Riel*; Coulter does not evade them but he does not focus them. There is, in short, a vagueness about the play that leaves readers and audiences wondering why it is worth their time. As critic Vincent Tovell observed in his review of the first production, 'The play presents many opinions about Riel and a good deal of evidence concerning him; it records him fully; but it does not interpret him' (*University of Toronto Quarterly*, vol. 20, 1950–1).

The two other plays in Coulter's Riel trilogy are slighter than *Riel*. *The Crime of Louis Riel* is a condensed, smaller-cast version of the main play, first produced in London, Ontario, in the 1966 Dominion Drama Festival, while *The Trial of Louis Riel* has been performed in Regina (where Riel was executed) each summer since 1967 as a tourist attraction.

Robertson Davies, who has recognized the importance of the Dominion Drama Festival, was also an active supporter and participant. Although his career as a playwright encompasses the early years of the new professionalism in Canadian theatre, much of his best work was written for amateur Little Theatres. *Overlaid* (a widely anthologized and performed play) and *Eros at Breakfast* won the Ottawa Drama League's annual playwriting competition in 1947 and 1948, and *Eros* was judged the best Canadian play at the 1948 DDF. *Fortune, My Foe* was similarly acclaimed in 1949—when Davies also won the DDF best director award for his Peterborough Little Theatre production of *The Taming of the Shrew*.

After his education at Upper Canada College, Queen's University, and Oxford University, Davies enjoyed a short acting career at London's Old Vic (where he worked under Tyrone Guthrie). When he returned to Canada in 1940 the contrast between the high culture of Europe and what he saw as the petty provincialism and repression of Canadian life became the subject of his early novels and plays. The puritanism of Ontario, symbolized by Ethel's wish for a family tombstone, is contrasted in the one-act play *Overlaid* with the freedom and universality of art represented by Pop's love of grand opera. In *Hope Deferred* (1949) a second early one-act play, an Indian girl, Chimène, must go to Paris to further her acting career when the Quebec clergy suppress a performance of Molière's *Tartuffe* in which she was to appear. Davies' first three-act play, *Fortune, My Foe* (1949), dramatizes the plight of Nicholas, who feels driven to leave an intellectually and culturally deprived Canada for an American university; he finally decides not to emigrate because of the example offered him by the European émigré Franz Szabo, a Bohemian puppet-maker. Although Szabo's puppet shows are based on European archetypes—Don Quixote, Dr Faustus—Szabo hopes to discover new themes, 'perhaps about Canada'. In *At My Heart's Core* (1950) the stranger Cantwell tempts three immigrants—Catherine Parr Traill, Susanna Moodie, and Frances Stewart—with visions of what they have given up in coming to Canada; the Old World, it is suggested, is far more open to love and art and achievement than Upper Canada in 1837. Given the pejorative connotation of Cantwell's name, and the spirited defence of their chosen lives by at least two of the women (Mrs Traill and Mrs Stewart), it is not entirely clear where Davies believes our sympathies should lie in this play. *At My Heart's Core* is, nonetheless, a substantial achievement, a comedy of 'high order' as *Canadian Forum* put it in March 1951.

There is a significant change in the plays, much influenced by Jungian theory, that Davies wrote in the 1950s: *A Jig for the Gypsy*, performed professionally at Toronto's Crest Theatre in 1954 and published the same year; *Hunting Stuart*, performed at the Crest in 1955, but not published until 1972; and *General Confession*, written in 1956, published in 1972, and not yet performed. The latter two especially dramatize journeys within the psyche. 'The theme of the portion of life that is unlived, for whatever reason,' Davies has written (in Geraldine Anthony's *Stage Voices*), 'has long appealed to me.' In *Hunting Stuart* Ben Stuart, a minor civil servant, finds the unlived portion of his life in the lusty and loved Bonnie Prince Charles. In *General Confession* Casanova, archetypal lover, is tried by the spirits he has raised—Voltaire (intellect), the Ideal Beloved (the anima), Cagliostro (the Shadow)—and triumphs because his life has been lived to the full, with style. In a key speech Casanova declares: 'God will know that in all the makeshifts of my life I have loved some things truly, held some things sacred, and that I have striven to give some pattern to the muddle of experience which the moving years have brought me.'

These themes of the revenge of the unlived life and the necessity to find cultural roots have a great deal to do with Davies' own discovery of Canada, a discovery dramatized in *Question Time* (1975), written immediately after the Deptford trilogy of novels, and produced by Toronto Arts Productions at the St Lawrence Centre in 1975. The central and traumatic incident of the second Deptford novel, *The Manticore*, occurs when David Staunton, led by a woman, Liesl, is forced to come to terms with his own innermost nature in the cave of the great historic bears in Switzerland. A similar incident is central to *Question Time*: here Davies examines the Canadian psyche, embodied in Peter Macadam, Prime Minister of Canada, who has undertaken a journey, not to the Old World but to Canada's Arctic, our Terra Incognita, where his plane crashes. Macadam discovers how seriously he has neglected his instinctive animal self when he 'becomes' the Great Bear, and ultimately comes to understand not only himself but the spirit of Canada represented by La Sorcière des Montagnes de Glace. She is, in the words of the play, 'the final reality; she is ourselves, our forebears, and our children; she is this land.'

Although Davies has secured international fame chiefly through his later novels, and is no longer an active force in Canadian theatre, his contribution to Canadian drama and theatre has been immense. He brought to his art a degree of professionalism not seen before in a Canadian dramatist. His plays are notable for the quality of their wit and satire, and, like Oliver Goldsmith, whom Davies has identified as the key influence on his drama, he writes sparkling dialogue and creates characters who are at once types, and yet keenly individualized. He shares with George Bernard Shaw the belief that drama should educate and not merely amuse. His dramatic *oeuvre* challenges the forces that stifle imagination and explores the human psyche in terms of psychology, history, myth, magic, and religion.

THE WORKERS' THEATRE

Davies and Coulter and most of the other playwrights who developed out of the Little Theatre movement and the Dominion Drama Festival were, by and large, conservative and traditional in their approach to theatre. They wrote for a middle-class audience that lacked the raucous energy of their nineteenth-century counterparts. Neither playwrights nor audiences were much interested in using the theatre as a forum for political discussion and agitation, despite the enormous economic and social problems faced by Canadians between the wars. The Dominion Drama Festival was therefore decidely nervous about plays that might threaten the Festival's dominant WASP social and political ethic. The 1930s saw the rise of theatre groups such as the Workers' Experimental Theatre and the Theatre of Action whose purpose was to promote theatre as an educational and political force. These groups wrote and produced plays with a radical emphasis that did not sit easily with organizers and patrons of the DDF. But one such work, Irwin Shaw's American anti-war play *Bury the Dead*, produced by Toronto's Theatre of Action, won its way to the 1937 finals in Ottawa. *Bury the Dead* was praised by adjudicator Michel St Denis for its experimentation but was passed over as a prize winner. This in itself proves little, perhaps, but members of the Theatre of Action company in Ottawa seem to have been treated by the Festival establishment as social and political delinquents. 'It was made fairly obvious to those of us who attended official functions that we were intruders,' Toby Ryan recalls. No one from Theatre of Action was invited to the final ball of the 1937 Festival, until the 'oversight' was corrected by Colonel Osborne, the Festival director.

The social peccadilloes of the Dominion Drama Festival could not, however, impede the growth of a significant body of Canadian political theatre in the 1930s. Almost exclusively the preserve of the political left, political theatre was promoted by Progressive Arts Clubs that were established in major Canadian cities in the 1930s. The aim of the PACs—as explained in their journal, *Masses* (1932–4) and elsewhere—was to develop a militant working-class art, literature, and theatre. For example, an offshoot of the Toronto PAC (established in 1932) was the Workers' Experimental Theatre whose actors were frequently unemployed workers who performed short plays and political skits (*Unemployment* by Trevor Maguire, *Looking Forward* by Frank Love, *Joe Derry* by Dorothy Livesay). Mounted in church basements, labour halls, and on picket lines, as well as in more conventional spaces such as Hart House Theatre, these plays offered crude but forceful ideological analyses of economic conditions and class structure (propaganda) in order to bring about a transformation of society (agitation). *Scientific Socialism* by N.W. Bowles is a typical piece of agitprop theatre. A worker in the play rejects the bourgeois nostrums of H.G. Wells and George Bernard Shaw: 'We are sick of the never-ending claptrap from poets and dramatists, carrying on a mimic battle with the critics,' he declares, while '*The cheering workers sweep off the stage, brushing G.B.S., H.G.W. and the policemen from their path.*'

The best of these political plays is *Eight Men Speak*, a full-length play by Oscar Ryan, Frank Love, Edward Cecil-Smith, and Mildred Goldberg based on the trial and imprisonment of eight Canadian communists and the attempted murder of Tim Buck, leader of the Communist Party of Canada, by a prison guard. Despite the fact that agitprop theatre championed political rather than aesthetic values, *Eight Men Speak* has a raw dramatic power and employs advanced structural and theatrical techniques foreign to the conventional, bourgeois Canadian stage. Because the conflict in the play is presented as social and political rather than personal, the authors use types not characters (Capitalism, Judge, Man in Cabaret); because there is a direct appeal to the audience, the play evokes the anti-illusionist theatre of Brecht. The close of Act IV provides a good example of Brecht's alienation effect (*Verfremdungseffekt*):

> All (*quietly but tensely*): Eight men speak!
> (*Here the blue border lights dim out and a full red light is flashed on scene.*)
> Buck: Smash Section 98!

All (*a little louder*): Eight men speak!
Popovich: Smash the iron heel!
All (*still more power in their voices, but very tensely*): Eight men speak!
All (*taking step forward and pointing through bars*): . . . to you!

New techniques include positional lighting ('spotlight dramaturgy'), episodic structure, and the use of multi-purpose representational stage props.

Eight Men Speak was performed at Toronto's Standard Theatre on 4 December 1933, with a cast of thirty-five unemployed workers and an audience of some 1,500. A second performance was suppressed by the Toronto police 'Red Squad', and a planned performance for Winnipeg's Walker Theatre was also prevented by police action. *Eight Men Speak* was not seen again until revived in Halifax by the Popular Projects Society in 1982.

The Workers' Theatre, with its combination of specifically Canadian concerns and international political and cultural links, had topical excitement and passion, and although it disappeared with the outbreak of the Second World War its vision and technique later resurfaced in the political style of George Luscombe's Toronto Workshop Productions, in the populist approach of Theatre Passe Muraille (one of whose trademarks is its striking use of stage props), and in the repertoire of Newfoundland's Mummers Troupe and other politically oriented companies.

RADIO DRAMA

Another key development in the 1930s in the creation of a national character and identity for Canadian drama was the formation in 1932 of the Canadian Radio Broadcasting Commission, which became in 1936 the Canadian Broadcasting Corporation. The decision to nationalize the Canadian National Railway's network of radio stations (formed in 1924–5) was a calculated effort to protect Canadians from the free-enterprise stations in the United States that regarded Canada as merely a natural extension of American territory, in the same way that American theatrical touring companies had regarded Canada as a natural extension of their circuits. Nationalization, which entailed state subsidization, meant that Canadian radio producers could systematically seek out and develop indigenous talent. The result was that between 1935 and 1965 the CBC became, in effect, Canada's 'National Repertory Theatre of the Air'; the extent of the patronage is suggested by the fact that (according to Howard Fink) the CBC employed some 1,300 playwrights in creating 'almost eight thousand drama broadcasts in the two decades from 1939 to the end of the golden age of Canadian radio. Some 3,500 of these were original Canadian plays.' (Very few, regrettably, have been published.) The professionalism demanded by the new medium influenced the work of many dramatists who also wrote for the stage, including Len Peterson, W.O. Mitchell, Mavor Moore, Patricia Joudry, George Ryga, David French, Michael Cook, Timothy Findley, and Sharon Pollock.

The first Canadian play to be broadcast was a piece called *The Rosary* (author unknown), aired by CNRA (Moncton) in 1925, followed in 1927 by the first regular series of broadcast plays in Canada, a weekly anthology produced on CNRV (Vancouver) by Jack Gillmore. Gillmore's series lasted four years and presented over one hundred plays, including new Canadian scripts. The first series of original Canadian plays on the national network was CNRM's 'The Romance of Canada' broadcast from Montreal in 1931–2, historical dramas on prominent Canadians by Merrill Denison, directed by Tyrone Guthrie. Even after the creation of the CRBC, private stations continued to produce important drama programs. Edmonton's CKUA, for example, ran one series from 1928 to 1941, commissioning new work from local playwrights such as Gwen Pharis Ringwood and Elsie Park Gowan. Gowan wrote over one hundred plays for radio, many of which were broadcast internationally. Prominent drama producers who began with private stations before moving to the CBC include Rupert Caplan who took over 'The Romance of Canada' series from Guthrie at CNRM before his appointment as Director of Drama for CBC Montreal in 1936—a position he held until 1968. In Winnipeg Esse Ljungh wrote and produced plays for CKY until he too joined the CBC, eventually succeeding the renowned Andrew Allan as the Corporation's National Supervisor of Drama in 1955.

Andrew Allan began his broadcasting career with CFRB in Toronto. After a period in England in the late 1930s he returned to Canada as

Director of Drama for CBC Vancouver and in 1943 was made the CBC's National Supervisor. From Toronto Allan launched two major national drama series: the 'Stage' series, which went on the air with 'Stage 44' in January 1944, and 'CBC Wednesday Night' in 1947. From the point of view of Canadian drama, 'Stage 44' developed into the more significant series. While 'CBC Wednesday Night' concentrated on the international repertoire (with some Canadian representation), the 'Stage' series featured the work of many Canadian playwrights during its twelve seasons of transmission—some of which, Allan once claimed, were second in popularity among listeners only to the Saturday night hockey broadcasts. Andrew Allan and his colleagues put Canada at the forefront of radio drama broadcasting. By developing and refining the acting, directing, and writing skills of Canadian artists, they helped prepare a body of talent that was essential to the establishment of a professional theatre in this country.

Among the small number of radio plays that have been published, the work of Len Peterson and Lister Sinclair stands out. Peterson's *Burlap Bags*, first broadcast by the CBC on 3 February 1946 (and later on CBC television), presents a compelling and deeply pessimistic view of post-war values: an intelligent and sensitive man is driven to suicide by a society whose members blind themselves (by wearing burlap bags over their heads) to greed, selfishness, and hypocrisy. Devoid of human caring, they imprison themselves in their own private worlds of 'duty' and 'responsibility':

> I was walking about in the city. . . . The walls of the buildings slanted inwardly, oppressively constricting their inhabitants. Office, home, store and factory, they were all alike. There were bars on many of the windows. Most of the people had shackles on their ankles chaining them to desks, and lathes, and kitchen stoves, and counters.

There is also a good deal of pessimism, along with some guarded optimism, in Lister Sinclair's plays. Twelve that were broadcast in the 1940s are collected in '*A Play on Words*' & *Other Radio Plays* (1948). Heavily influenced by the Second World War, they display a wide range of subject matter and dramatic structure. *Day of Victory*, for example, although it relies on a Narrator—as Sinclair's plays frequently do—rather than intrinsic action to carry the story line, is a powerful plea for continued opposition to the ideology of Nazi Germany. *No Scandal in Spain* is a monologue of a Spanish prisoner who has spoken out against Franco's fascism and is given the opportunity to commit suicide rather than face the 'scandal' of a court martial; the tension created by the prisoner's uncertainty about what to do—he is given only thirty minutes to decide—is central to the play's success. On the other hand, Sinclair's propensity for using drama simply to *lecture* to his listeners ruins many of his plays, however well-intentioned the lecture. *You Can't Stop Now*, for example, advocates world government as a means of preventing atomic warfare—an admirable idea. But having a Narrator simply tell radio listeners what they must do to promote this—'Sit down now, this minute, and write a letter to your member of parliament, another one to the prime minister, and another one to the newspapers. That'll do to go on with; if you really want to, you can send some telegrams and do some ''phoning'' too. But you must write those letters'—destroys dramatic credibility.

'A Play on Words' & Other Radio Plays also contains a propanganda piece encouraging new immigrants to accept Canada as their home, an Oedipus play, a biography of J.S. Bach, a documentary drama about cancer, an educational drama about Canada for US listeners, a farce about Toronto ('Canada's National Joke'), and another war monologue. In addition, the collection usefully provides cast lists for the original broadcasts, which underlines the importance of radio in providing employment and experience for actors such as John Drainie, Jane Mallett, Lorne Greene, Don Harron, Robert Christie, and others. Among the actors who were later to develop through radio drama were Frances Hyland, William Shatner, John Colicos, and Christopher Plummer.

After the slow decline of radio drama productions (and listeners) in the 1950s and 1960s—caused by the advent of television and the rise of professional theatre—a resurgence occurred in the 1980s under the leadership of the CBC's Susan Rubes. While an audience for radio drama still exists, and actors, directors, and playwrights are still attracted by the medium, it is clear that radio drama will never again occupy the vital place in the cultural life of Canada that it enjoyed in the 1930s and 1940s.

DRAMA AND THE UNIVERSITIES

Another aspect of Canada's efforts to forge a national theatrical identity was the role played by the universities and, in particular, by the Banff School of Fine Arts. The first Chair of Drama at a Canadian university (the first, in fact, at a Commonwealth university) was established at the University of Saskatchewan in 1945. It was held by Emrys Maldwyn Jones, who envisioned a major role for university drama departments in supporting a National Theatre for Canada. In an essay published in *Culture* in 1946, he explained his concept of a National Theatre, and the universities' responsibilities towards it.

> A National Theatre is not a building, nor a museum, nor just a collection of works: It is an idea and an activity. It is the enthusiastic work of many clubs, theatres, schools and universities from coast to coast, each expressing itself independently in its own way, yet all united by a common desire. This common desire must be concerned with the expression and development of a truly Canadian culture through the medium of the Drama. Since such a cultural expression presupposes its own literature, the writing of Canadian plays must be a most important function of this National Theatre.

The universities, however, were slow to respond to the challenge of participating in the 'expression and development of a truly Canadian culture through the medium of Drama'—much slower than their American counterparts. Queen's University and the University of Alberta established Departments of Drama in 1947, but the main development in Canadian university drama education had to wait until the 1960s. By then much pioneering work had been accomplished, particularly in Western Canada, at both the high-school and post-secondary level. One of the most important steps had been taken by the University of Alberta. Before it opened a Department of Drama, the university, through its Extension Department, set up in 1933 what was originally described as 'a school in the arts related to the theatre' in Banff, Alberta. The Banff School of Fine Arts, as it soon came to be known (now the Banff Centre School of Fine Arts), later broadened its mandate to include the teaching of a broad range of literature and the arts, but its interest in theatre remained strong. The first head of the theatre program, Elizabeth Sterling Haynes, initiated a pattern of inviting leading European and American teachers and artists to Banff. It was one such visitor—Frederick Koch, a professor at the University of North Carolina and founder of 'America's Folk Theatre', the Carolina Playmakers, in 1918—who was a major influence on Gwen Pharis Ringwood, the most important playwright associated with Banff in the 1930s and 1940s. Along with Merrill Denison, Herman Voaden, John Coulter, and Robertson Davies, Ringwood was one of the key figures in the creation of a national dramatic literature.

After studies at the University of Alberta (where she wrote plays for radio station CKUA), Ringwood went in 1937 to the University of North Carolina, where Koch's guidance (and the example of American folk playwright Paul Green) impressed upon her the potential for plays about the people of the Canadian prairies. Four of the five plays she wrote at this time were produced by the Carolina Playmakers— *Chris Axelson, Blacksmith*, *Still Stands the House*, *Pasque Flower*, and *One Man's House*. The fifth, *Dark Harvest* (a revised version of *Pasque Flower*), was not performed until 1945. Two of these plays— the one-act *Still Stands the House* and the full-length *Dark Harvest*— are tragedies that have strong claims to being Canadian classics. *Still Stands the House* is a grim and powerful metaphor of Canadian life in the Depression years when drought turned much of the prairies into a dust bowl. The blizzards of winter and the droughts of summer are Ringwood's images of a derangement in Nature mirroring the disorder within the human world of the Warren household. Within that farm household are Hester, who represents a hard, puritanical, pioneer past, and Ruth, the portent of a more graceful future—two antagonists fated to clash with tragic inevitability. *Dark Harvest* is an equally sensitive depiction of prairie environment and character—novelist Margaret Laurence has called it a 'timeless play', comparing the character of its protagonist, Gerth Hansen, to those in the novels of Frederick Grove, Sinclair Ross, and Martha Ostenso—though the play suffers from stilted dialogue and a contrived ending.

Ringwood's association with Banff led to the production of a group of her comedies there in the early 1940s. *The Courting of Marie Jenvrin* is a bland but technically adroit play about a young woman's schemes to bring fresh cream to Yellowknife, but *The Jack and the Joker* deserves much wider recognition than it has received. There is satiric bite in this play's exposure of the bigotry and small-mindedness of rural Alberta; and the skulduggery of an ambitious politician is admirably pinpointed. *The Rainmaker*—about a professional rainmaker hired by the citizens of Medicine Hat, Alberta, to end a drought—introduces a wide variety of outlandish characters but shows a sentimental vein that deprives it of the vigour of *The Jack and the Joker*. Another comedy, *Widger's Way*, was performed at the University of Alberta in 1952. Judged by W.J. Keith to be Ringwood's finest achievement—'a sparkling if brittle theatrical gem'—*Widger's Way* celebrates the irrational, the illogical, and the absurd. Its zany murder investigation does not merely *remind* us of the plays of Tom Stoppard, it *matches* Stoppard, falling short only in its submission—again—to a sentimental conclusion.

Ringwood's contact with the Indian tribes of the Williams Lake area of northern British Columbia where she lived from 1953 until her death in 1984 may have reinforced her strong sympathy for outsiders (many of her plays dramatize the loneliness and fears of immigrant groups). Her 'Indian' trilogy—*Lament for Harmonica* (or *Maya*), *The Stranger*, and *The Furies*, not produced as a trilogy until 1982—represents a powerful indictment of white society's treatment of British Columbia's native peoples. In *Lament for Harmonica* Maya kills an Indian who loves her to save the white father of her child. *The Stranger* is a harrowing tragedy dominated by images of gelding, infanticide, murder, suicide, and madness. Jana, a chief's daughter, has been wronged by her white common-law husband, father of her child. When the white woman, Barbara, gelds Jana's stallion and steals her husband, Jana poisons Barbara, then kills herself and her daughter. The play uses many of the themes and theatrical conventions Ringwood had been experimenting with in earlier plays—chorus, chanting, drumming, the use of Indian speech, and a heightened sense of language. *The Furies* is a short yet complex play combining two plots. One takes place in the past when four young Indian girls who had been seduced by a common lover, the foreign Jacques LaRange, hang themselves, thereby driving him into madness—much as the Furies in Greek legend drove wrongdoers to madness and death. The second plot concerns the rape and murder of a young Indian girl and the castration of her murderer by three old Indian women (the Furies of the title).

George Ryga—once Ringwood's student in playwriting in Banff—

has praised her for creating a deeper awareness of the richness of Canadian mythology. He has also castigated Canadian theatres for neglecting Ringwood's plays, complaining of 'the dereliction of responsibility by our large regional theatres in not displaying a concern . . . in preserving our heritage and the foundations of our national theatrical development.' His point is well taken, but it is also true that during some of Ringwood's most productive years very little in the way of professional theatre—regional or otherwise—existed in Canada. The process of establishing a national theatrical identity had been achieved almost exclusively in the context of *amateur* activity. CBC radio, of course, was in every sense a professional organization, but live theatre in Canada from the end of the touring and stock era to the early 1950s was predominantly amateur. The next crucial phase consisted of moving from that amateur achievement to a fully professional status.

ANTHONY, GERALDINE, ed. *Stage Voices. Twelve Canadian Playwrights Talk about Their Lives and Work*. Toronto, Doubleday, 1978.

COULTER, JOHN. *In My Day: Memoirs*. Willowdale, Ontario, Hounslow Press, 1980.

FINK, HOWARD. 'A National Radio Drama in English.' *Contemporary Canadian Theatre: New World Visions*, ed. Anton Wagner. Toronto, Simon & Pierre, 1985.

KEITH, W.J. *Canadian Literature in English*. London and New York, Longman, 1985.

LAURENCE, MARGARET. Foreword to *The Collected Plays of Gwen Pharis Ringwood*, ed. Enid Delgatty Rutland. Ottawa, Borealis Press, 1982.

MITCHELL, ROY. *Creative Theatre*. 2nd ed. New York, Kindle Press, 1969.

RYAN, TOBY GORDON. *Stage Left. Canadian Theatre in the Thirties: A Memoir*. Toronto, CTR Publications, 1981.

RYGA, GEORGE. Preface to *The Collected Plays of Gwen Pharis Ringwood*, ed. Enid Delgatty Rutland. Ottawa, Borealis Press, 1982.

STUART, E. ROSS. *The History of Prairie Theatre. The Development of Theatre in Alberta, Manitoba and Saskatchewan 1833–1982*. Toronto, Simon & Pierre, 1984.

TERRISS, ELLALINE. *Ellaline Terriss, by Herself and with Others*. London, Cassell, 1928.

WRIGHT, RICHARD and ROBIN ENDRES, eds. *Eight Men Speak and Other Plays from the Canadian Workers' Theatre*. Toronto, New Hogtown Press, 1976.

Preparing for the first rehearsal at the first Stratford Festival, 1953.
First row, from left: Irene Worth, Robert Goodier, Bruce Swerdfager, Amelia Hall.
Second row, from left: Timothy Findley, William Needles, Eric House, William
Hutt, Roland Bull, Robert Christie, Douglas Rain, Richard Robinson, Alex Smith,
Betty Leighton. Back row, seated: Elspeth Chisholm, John Hayes. (Photo: Peter
Smith and Co., Stratford.)

3

CANADIAN PROFESSIONAL THEATRE:
GROWTH AND DEVELOPMENT

GOVERNMENT AND THEATRE

Before the Canada Council was created in 1957 theatre had to survive without the benefit of government support. As an amateur activity it could and did; professional companies, however, were much more difficult to sustain. One such company was the John Holden Players. Founded by John Holden in 1934 as the Actors' Colony in the small Muskoka, Ontario, resort town of Bala, by 1937 the company was operating a professional year-round repertory system—summers in Muskoka, fall and winter in Winnipeg, and spring in Toronto. CBC Radio broadcast some of the company's productions from Muskoka in 1939, but the outbreak of war interrupted their activities and finally made it impossible to continue. In 1946 Sydney Risk founded the Everyman Theatre Company in Vancouver and ran a successful and sometimes innovative repertoire (including children's plays) for seven years. This group's production early in 1953 of the sexually frank *Tobacco Road*, a controversial American play by Jack Kirkland based on the Erskine Caldwell novel, was closed by the police (they arrested members of the cast onstage during a performance) and the resulting litigation led Risk to close his venture.

At about the time that Risk was opening the Everyman in Vancouver, Dora Mavor Moore—a Glaswegian raised and educated in Toronto and trained as an actress at London's RADA—was forming the New Play Society in Toronto. A non-profit but professional group, the

NPS opened in October 1946 in the Royal Ontario Museum Theatre with a production of John Millington Synge's *The Playboy of the Western World*. Unlike the Actors' Colony and the Everyman Theatre the NPS produced many Canadian plays. No unsubsidized professional theatre before or since can match NPS's record in this regard. Lister Sinclair's *The Man in the Blue Moon*, performed in May 1947, was the first NPS Canadian play, followed by works by Mavor Moore (Dora Mavor Moore's son), Andrew Allan, Morley Callaghan, Mazo de la Roche, and Harry Boyle. The première of John Coulter's epic *Riel* in February 1950 was one of NPS's most notable achievements. NPS continued to be active throughout the 1950s and 1960s, operating a theatre school, producing the famous *Spring Thaw* reviews, and mounting special events such as an all-Canadian play festival in 1965, before closing in 1971.

Other professional companies in the 1950s include Toronto's Jupiter and Crest Theatres, which opened in 1951 and 1954 respectively. Like the NPS, Jupiter initially used the ROM theatre, but despite its high-quality productions (with actors such as John Drainie, Lorne Greene, and Christopher Plummer), and the inclusion of Canadian plays in its repertoire, it survived only until 1954. The Crest, founded by brothers Donald and Murray Davis, had a longer life. It opened in an 822-seat theatre on Mt Pleasant Road on 5 January 1954 with a production of *Richard of Bordeaux* by Gordon Daviot (Josephine Tey) starring Murray Davis. When it closed in April 1966 it had amply fulfilled its stated intention of 'providing opportunities for the development of Canadian artists, directors, playwrights, designers and technicians'. While its repertoire was international it produced plays by Canadian playwrights Robertson Davies, Ted Allen, John Gray, Mary Jukes, Marcel Dubé, Mavor Moore, and Bernard Slade; its directors included Herbert Whittaker, Henry Caplan, Robert Gill, Douglas Campbell, John Holden, Malcolm Black, Barry Morse, Mavor Moore, Leon Major, Jean Roberts, Powys Thomas, David Gardner, Allan Lund, Kurt Reis, Marigold Charlesworth, John Hirsch, Donald Davis, and George McCowan. It nourished a new generation of young Canadian actors—Amelia Hall, Richard Monette, John Vernon, George Luscombe, Jane Mallett, Frances Hyland, Leo Ciceri, Jackie Burroughs, Martha Henry, Eric House, Kate Reid, and Charmion King.

A second objective—'To provide repertory theatre in Toronto comparable with the best of British repertory companies'—was irregularly achieved but there were memorable productions: a 1954 première of Robertson Davies' *A Jig for the Gypsy* starring Barbara Chilcott (the Davises' sister) as Benoni; a 1956 production of Chekhov's *The Three Sisters* with Amelia Hall, Charmion King, and Kate Reid; a 1961 production of Samuel Beckett's *Krapp's Last Tape* with Donald Davis fresh from acclaim in the role of Krapp in New York.

Because the Crest came to rely too heavily perhaps on government subsidy it suffered badly when in 1964 the Canada Council refused to approve a requested grant of $20,000 and the Ontario Arts Council approved only $10,000 of a $30,000 application. A press release issued by the Canada Council justified its refusal on the grounds that the Crest had not done enough 'to improve its standards, its financial prospects, or the size of its audience'. The company survived for another two years, finally closing on 30 April 1966 with a production of Ibsen's *Hedda Gabler* starring Marilyn Lightstone and, fittingly, directed by Murray Davis. Reviewing the Crest's history Ross Stuart has written: '. . . to dismiss the Crest is to dismiss an entire generation of the Canadian theatre. . . . Without the generation nurtured there, without the Crest, theatre in Toronto today would be different.'

The Crest opened before the Canada Council existed, but eventually became dependent on government support. A comparable pattern developed with the best-known of all Canadian theatres, the Stratford Shakespearean Festival. Now one of the world's major theatre organizations with an annual budget (in 1986) in excess of thirteen million dollars, comprising $8,825,358 of box office revenue, $2,284,170 of private fund-raising, and $1,917,000 of direct government subsidy ($784,000 from the Canada Council, $1,133,000 from the Ontario Arts Council), it began somewhat more modestly in 1953. Founder Tom Patterson and his colleagues attempted to raise just $150,000 to mount Tyrone Guthrie's first season of *Richard III* and *All's Well That Ends Well* in a 1,477-seat tent. Of that $150,000, only $10,000 came from government: $5,000 from the Province of Ontario and an equal amount from the City of Stratford. Much larger sums were given for the construction of a permanent theatre in 1957 ($250,000 each from the provincial and federal governments), and the first Canada Council grant of $10,000 was also allocated to the Stratford

Festival in 1957. Stratford's Elizabethan open stage, designed by Tanya Moiseiwitsch, has justly become famous, inspiring similar designs at the Chichester Festival in England and the Guthrie Theatre in Minneapolis. Seating 2,262 (in 1987) in a 220 degree circle (with no spectator more than sixty-five feet from the stage), the Festival Theatre is complemented by the more conventional proscenium Avon Theatre and the experimental Third Stage.

The extensive funding that eventually became available to Stratford and other theatres arose from a federal government initiative in 1949 to appoint a Royal Commission on National Development in the Arts, Letters, and Sciences. Chaired by Vincent Massey, the Commission spent two years consulting experts in a variety of disciplines as well as hearing witnesses from many walks of life. Robertson Davies presented a submission in the form of a dramatic dialogue in which two characters named Lovewit and Trueman make a number of pertinent observations and recommendations—on the need for professionalism if the 'full and unmistakable power' of theatre is to be realized in Canada, on the importance of higher critical standards, and on the values of proper theatrical education and training. Underlying the entire dialogue is the hope—the assumption, even—that 'a robust Canadian theatre would bring forth a large body of Canadian plays, some of them good enough for export.'

When the Commission submitted its report in 1951 one recommendation—of inestimable future influence on theatre and the arts in general in Canada—was that 'a body be created to be known as the Canada Council for the Encouragement of the Arts, Letters, Humanities and Social Sciences. . . .' The recommendation was accepted, and the Canada Council was created by an Act of Parliament in March 1957. With an initial endowment of $50 million, supplemented in subsequent years by annual grants (the total Canada Council budget for 1987-8 was $88,444,000), the Council was able to make significant sums of public money available for Canadian theatre—$15,713,000 in 1987-8, excluding grants to individual dramatists and special grants under the Explorations program (experimental work in the arts) funded at $2,630,000.

It has been suggested by Jerry Wasserman that the formation of the Canada Council changed 'the nature of theatre in Canada more than any other single development, providing a sudden massive influx of government funding for buildings, companies and individuals engaged in the arts.' Though the impact of Canada Council funding was immediate, extraordinary, and enduring, it would be a mistake to credit the Council exclusively with providing the impetus for the rapid and successful growth of professional theatre in Canada since the Second World War. CBC Radio, as we have seen, made an important contribution to theatre through the opportunities it gave playwrights, actors, and directors to develop their careers. Television, too, provided opportunities and challenges for many actors (Douglas Rain, Frances Hyland, Tony Van Bridge, Leo Ciceri, and others) and directors, as well as designers. Playwrights who had written for radio (Lister Sinclair, Len Peterson, Mavor Moore, for example) also wrote television plays and some playwrights who became prominent in the professional theatre have also written for television. George Ryga's *Indian* was produced on CBC's 'Quest' series in 1962, and Carol Bolt's plays were seen on series such as 'Front Row Centre' and 'Performance' in the 1970s. CBC Television has also produced adaptations of Canadian stage plays: Linda Griffiths' *Maggie and Pierre*, David Fennario's *Balconville*, and John Gray's *Billy Bishop Goes to War* have reached large national audiences through television.

No one would argue that an infusion of money—no matter on how Maecenean a scale—can of itself bring about a cultural movement of national importance. It may, however, provide the conditions for it—as, arguably, the economic wealth of Periclean Athens, Augustan Rome, Elizabethan England, or Vienna at the end of the eighteenth century provided the conditions that gave us key cultural moments in the development of Western civilization. In 1960 money became available to create Montreal's bilingual National Theatre School, and a chain of major professional theatres, funded mainly from federal and provincial government sources, rapidly emerged. In Winnipeg a merger of the Winnipeg Little Theatre and a semi-professional group, Theatre 77, enabled John Hirsch and Tom Hendry to found the Manitoba Theatre Centre in 1958, the first of the country's large regional theatres. Others followed: the Vancouver Playhouse and the Neptune Theatre in Halifax in 1963, the Citadel in Edmonton in 1965, Regina's Globe in 1966; the Saidye Bronfman Centre in Montreal in 1967; Theatre Calgary and Theatre New Brunswick in 1968; Toronto's St Lawrence Centre in 1970. The National Arts Centre

(1969)—rivalled only by Edmonton's Citadel as the most grandiose of these complexes—contains two theatres and an opera house built at a cost of over $46 million. In addition, the Shaw Festival at Niagara-on-the-Lake was inaugurated in 1962 (and built a new theatre in 1973), the Charlottetown Festival in Prince Edward Island began in 1964, and an Arts and Culture Centre opened in St John's, Newfoundland, in 1967.

Clearly, such massive capital ventures—and associated operating expenses—would have been impossible without government support. At the end of the theatre-building boom, however, it was appropriate to ask what, precisely, had been achieved by such support? Certainly there were many more theatres in the country, and they were infinitely better equipped for productions, and considerably more comfortable for audiences. Many more plays could be produced, and many more artistic challenges and opportunities were there for Canadian actors, directors, designers, and technicians. But what of Robertson Davies' hope for Canadian *plays*? To what extent had Canadian playwrights benefited from the spending spree? Was the Canadian playwright an essential component of the now-bustling theatrical culture, or still—as in the nineteenth century—only an occasional, barely noticed, participant, jostled to the periphery again by theatrical imports?

THE LESSONS OF 1967:
JOHN HERBERT, JAMES REANEY, GEORGE RYGA

Amid the hoop-la of the 1967 Centennial celebrations there were three productions of new Canadian plays that, while important in themselves, also suggest something in general about the direction Canadian theatre was to take in the 1960s and 1970s. On 23 February 1967 John Herbert's prison drama, *Fortune and Men's Eyes*, opened at the Actor's Playhouse in New York City. Later that year, on 25 July, at Stratford's Avon Theatre, James Reaney's *Colours in the Dark* had its première; and towards the end of the year, on 23 November, George Ryga's new play, *The Ecstasy of Rita Joe*, was produced by the Vancouver Playhouse.

At the suggestion of Robertson Davies, Herbert sent *Fortune and Men's Eyes* to Douglas Campbell at Stratford. Campbell was impressed, so much so that he helped arrange a workshop production there in

October 1965. Directed by Bruno Gerussi, the production (featuring Richard Monette and other young members of the Stratford company) made no further progress at Stratford, its subject matter and language being judged unsuitable for Stratford audiences. It was left for a New York company to mount the first full production—and a New York publisher, Grove Press, to bring out the first edition in 1967—of what remains one of Canada's most powerful modern plays. The first full Canadian professional production did not take place until 1975, at the Phoenix Theatre, Toronto, when it won the Chalmers Award as best Canadian play of the Toronto season. It has received many productions outside Canada, and it has also been made into a feature film.

Fortune and Men's Eyes draws on Herbert's own self-proclaimed homosexuality and on his experiences in a Canadian reformatory (Guelph) where he was incarcerated for six months when he was twenty, on a charge of gross indecency (a charge he has always denied). In its stagecraft and sense of theatre the play is no fluke; Herbert studied acting, directing, and production at the New Play Society School of Drama from 1955 to 1958, and took another two years' training as a dancer with the School of the National Ballet of Canada. Between 1960 and 1964 he was artistic director of Adventure Theatre, Toronto, and later of the New Venture Players, Toronto.

While *Fortune and Men's Eyes* speaks directly to issues relating to homosexuality and the brutality of prison life, it is primarily concerned with human relationships and how four young men come to terms with the injustices of their childhood, denial of love, and consequent degradation. The play focuses on the 'education' of a new inmate, Smitty, and on his eventual corruption. His education is conducted by three fellow inmates: Rocky, a dangerous pimp and homosexual; Queenie, a transvestite, 'coarse, cruel, tough and voluptuously pretty'; and Mona, an epicene youth of eighteen and repeated victim of gang rape, whose stoicism and sensitivity represent a possible hope for Smitty. In the course of the play Smitty is raped by Rocky, sexually dominated by Queenie and, in turn, attempts to seduce Mona. In the final scene Mona, a Christlike figure, is being whipped by a guard (offstage) while Smitty, now given over to violence and a criminal future, addresses the audience directly: 'I'll pay you all back'.

Although the play's themes are tough and unpalatable, Herbert seasons them with energy, humour, and subtlety. Queenie is a corrupt character (a creature from Céline or Genet), but 'she' is richly human in her capacity to survive and in her earthy bawdiness. Her Christmas drag routine is sure-fire theatre and acts unobtrusively as ironic commentary on Mona's aborted 'quality of mercy' speech from the trial scene in *The Merchant of Venice*. The other important Shakespearean reference in *Fortune and Men's Eyes*—sonnet 29, which gives the play its title—is also deeply ironic. Its notion of 'sweet love remembered' as an antidote to despair and self-pity contrasts starkly with the only kind of 'love' recognized in this prison—coarse physical gratification. The possibility of some kind of redemptive love—such as that offered by Mona to Smitty—is reinforced by a web of imagery related to birds and flight, first seen in the overture when a boys' choir sings 'Alouette' and followed through to sonnet 29:

> Haply I think on thee, and then my soul
> (Like to the lark at break of day arising,
> From sullen earth) sings hymns at heaven's gate.

The reflective language of the sonnet—and of Mona's speeches—is juxtaposed with the raw, scatological, and often brutal language of the other characters: 'All Indians is screwin' finks an' stoolies, an' I woulden trust 'em with a bottle o' cheap shavin' lotion; and that Blackfeet bum probably slugged some ol' fairy in a public crapper, t' git a bottle o' wine.' Such speeches (this one is by Rocky) are unpleasant, but they are nonetheless vital and rich, a poetry of the down-and-outs that compels attention.

Unfortunately John Herbert is an all-too-common literary phenomenon—a writer known primarily for a single work. He has written a number of plays, including *Omphale and the Hero* (1974) and the four short plays in *Some Angry Summer Songs* (1976), but they lack the authenticity, urgency, and craftsmanship that characterize *Fortune and Men's Eyes*. The plot of *Omphale and the Hero* reads like a parody of a Tennessee Williams play. The ageing French-Canadian whore Antoinette, a former librarian, becomes infatuated with a young drifter, Mac. He falls in love (improbably) with another woman and Antoinette is murdered by one of her regular customers, the police chief, as stereotyped a villain as any in Canadian melodrama. In a scene memorable for its gratuitous offensiveness, the town mayor works himself into sexual orgasm at full centre stage.

If the Stratford Festival ignored an opportunity to promote an important Canadian play in the case of *Fortune and Men's Eyes*— even after spending some time and effort in initially encouraging its author—it partly redeemed itself with its support of James Reaney's *Colours in the Dark*. Before turning to playwriting, Reaney had distinguished himself as a poet, winning Governor General's Awards for his first two volumes of poetry, *The Red Heart* (1949) and *A Suit of Nettles* (1958). Reaney's own sense of literary history would have told him that the transition from the private world of poetry to the public world of the stage would be a difficult one. And it was. Although his first volume of plays, *The Killdeer and Other Plays* (1962), won another Governor General's Award, the attempt to stage his stylized and archetypal situations divorced from conventional characterization, dialogue, and plot meets with strictly limited success. Early plays such as *The Killdeer*, *The Sun and the Moon*, and *The Easter Egg* (which was revived by Stratford for a 1970 spring tour production at the National Arts Centre) are enlivened by bold imagination, outlandish figures, and poetic fancy, but too often succumb to far-fetched situations, melodramatic resolutions, and dramatic effects that, as W.J. Keith has said, 'are poised on the razor's edge between imaginative charm and irritating silliness'.

Listen to the Wind (1972), first performed in 1966, pursues Reaney's interest in the images and values of childhood, though this play is also heavily melodramatic. The same interest is further developed in his first major achievement for the theatre, *Colours in the Dark* (1969), directed in its Stratford première by John Hirsch. Like Henry Beissel's striking play, *Inook and the Sun* (1974), *Colours in the Dark* has quickly established itself as a classic of Canadian children's theatre that also appeals to adults. In *Colours* Reaney still dispenses almost entirely with plot, characterization, motivation, and conventional structure, replacing them with structural motifs related to the thematic considerations of the play: the letters of the alphabet, the books of the Bible, the seasons. Central to these motifs is the archetypal theme of a Fall and possible Redemption. Put this way the play sounds pretentious, academic; but this is not the case. The temptation of our Grand Parents by Satan becomes the farcical scene where Pa and Ma discover that a snake has joined them in bed. Only the unobtrusive author's note, 'ruin original', reveals Reaney's collocation of Milton's Adam and Eve and his own Canadian Ma and Pa. The play's conclusion, where the Kid unwraps his eyes and discovers that he has recovered from his illness and that Spring has come, shows a dramatic inevitability far removed from the contrived happy ending of melodrama. But the key structural element of *Colours in the Dark* that provides coherence to the multiple incidents and to the rapid switches from one mood to another is the poems that Reaney deploys throughout the play and that are themselves given coherence by the central 'Existence' poem. And what fine poems they are—Reaney plunders his twenty years of poetry to create a memorable play.

Having previously relied mainly on amateur companies to produce his work, Reaney was fortunate that the resources of the Stratford Festival were available to reveal the qualities of *Colours in the Dark*. But, like the case of *Fortune and Men's Eyes*, this was not to be a sign of an enduring and mutually rewarding association between the Festival and Canada's playwrights. No Herbert or Reaney play has subsequently been produced at Stratford, and the record of the Festival's encouragement of Canadian playwrights is, on the whole, dismal. In the early 1960s there were some workshop productions of original Canadian plays, and in 1961 even a mainstage presentation of a new work by Canadian Donald Jack—a comedy called *The Canvas Barricade* that received critical praise but little box-office support. Tom Hendry's *Satyricon* at the Avon in 1969 was neither an artistic nor a financial success; however, Larry Fineberg's *Eve*, an adaptation of Constance Beresford-Howe's novel *The Book of Eve*, starring Jessica Tandy, was successful both artistically and financially at the Avon during the 1976 season and subsequently played in England, the United States, and Holland. In 1972 an all-Canadian repertoire was presented at the Third Stage, which has also mounted plays by Henry Beissel, Michael Ondaatje, Sheldon Rosen, Larry Fineberg, Tom Cone, and Sharon Pollock. Cone also adapted Carlo Goldoni's *Servant of Two Masters* (Avon, 1980), and John Murrell provided new adaptations of Chekhov's *Uncle Vanya* and *The Seagull* for productions at the Avon and Festival theatres in 1978 and 1980 respectively. Credit for the higher profile accorded Canadian playwrights at Stratford in the later 1970s must go to artistic director Robin Phillips and his literary manager Urjo Kareda, who subsequently became artistic director of Toronto's Tarragon Theatre. Since the departure of Phillips and Kareda in 1980 Canadian plays and playwrights have not been among Stratford's priorities. Despite the artistic and financial risks involved in presenting unfamiliar Canadian plays to conservative audiences, Stratford (which has on occasion described itself as Canada's 'National' theatre) could do much more to develop Canadian drama. Compared, for example, to Britain's Royal Shakespeare Company (which, admittedly, receives a proportionately far higher government subsidy than Stratford), Stratford's record of support for its country's playwrights reveals little courage or initiative.

James Reaney has written several other plays since *Colours in the Dark*. None of them have been produced by the Stratford Festival, though one, *King Whistle!* (about labour unrest in Stratford in the 1930s), was performed in November 1979 at the Avon Theatre. *Gyroscope*, a 1981 Tarragon Theatre production, is similar in tone (satiric) and subject matter (small-town life), to his earlier work, but *Wacousta!* (workshopped in London and Timmins, Ontario, in 1978) and *The Canadian Brothers* (performed by University of Calgary students in 1983) were inspired by the nineteenth-century melodramatic novels of Major John Richardson.

But it is his trilogy of plays—collectively known as *The Donnellys*—about the notorious south-western Ontario family murdered in 1880 that has solidified Reaney's reputation as one of Canada's most important playwrights. Developed in collaboration with director Keith Turnbull, and presented at the Tarragon Theatre between 1973 and 1975 (followed by a national tour), the trilogy is widely considered to be among the finest of Canadian theatrical achievements. It combines history, folktales, myth, music, dancing, mime, and a host of ingenious theatrical techniques and devices. The strength of the first part, *Sticks and Stones*, lies in its exhilarating celebration of living and dying; charged with energy and passion, it is as much a documentary of rural life—like a novel by George Eliot—as an explanation of why the Donnellys died. But precisely when Reaney seeks to win our sympathy for the Donnellys—to justify them—the play loses its hold on us. It is an imposition to ask us to believe that the Donnellys are killed because they do not vote Tory. The reason for their death is in the text: Donnelly (like all the men of his family) is a god, a king, and the king must die in the same way that the seasons must change, and the barley must be threshed to become whisky to be pissed against the wall. Historical explanation is at odds with the play's archetypal assertions. The Donnellys are outsiders, cursed, unexplainable, like Oedipus or the Ancient Mariner.

Crucial weaknesses in the trilogy arise from Reaney's excesses: too many characters, too many incidents, too many places, too many styles. This becomes virulent in Parts II and III, *The St. Nicholas Hotel* and *Handcuffs*. Compression gives way to diffuseness, the mythic to the naturalistic, immediate presentation to historical flashback, drama to documentary. We protest when our view of the Donnellys is obstructed by some eighty characters, when we are given detailed geography lessons on Perth County, the history of the local stage lines, the story of Finnegan's wedding cake, even the story of how Mary Donovan lost her cow.

Yet if the trilogy is a victim of Reaney's excesses, it is also the beneficiary of his bold and exuberant imagination and his astute craftsmanship. His carefully arranged array of images throughout the text is given heightened impact in production—the full effect of *The Donnellys* can be appreciated only in production—through visual manifestation of ladders, sticks, stones, handcuffs, wheels, and spinning tops, all helping to bind together this multi-faceted and complex work. The characters are too often merely figures from melodrama, yet few are tiresome; many are engaging, some unforgettable. And it says much for Reaney's skill that he is able so adroitly to enmesh large symbolic patterns of life and death with the urgent human and social issues of bigotry, prejudice, and hatred as reflected in a small Ontario community towards the end of the last century.

After he had seen Part II, *The St. Nicholas Hotel*, Urjo Kareda looked forward to the day when the whole trilogy might be performed together—'perhaps,' as he optimistically put it, 'under the banner of the Stratford Festival' (*Toronto Star*, 18 November 1974). Stratford did not respond to the challenge—even when Kareda was literary manager there—but audiences did have the opportunity of seeing the trilogy performed under the auspices of Keith Turnbull's NDWT Company on the 1975 national tour, culminating in a one-day nine-hour extravaganza at Toronto's Bathurst St Theatre on 14 December 1975—a Canadian *Nicholas Nickleby* five years before the Royal Shakespeare Company thought of it.

The third key production of a Canadian play in 1967 was of George Ryga's *The Ecstasy of Rita Joe* at the Vancouver Playhouse on 23 November. The Playhouse had opened in 1963 with an Irish play, Brendan Behan's *The Hostage*, but under the 1964–7 artistic directorship of Malcolm Black some new Canadian plays were produced. The boldest step in this direction was taken by Joy Coghill, who succeeded Black in 1967.

In commissioning and producing *Rita Joe*, the Playhouse took a significant risk, for Ryga was not at that time an experienced playwright, though in 1962 his one-act play *Indian*, about an encounter between a dispossessed, unnamed Indian and a civil servant from the Indian Affairs Department, was produced on CBC television. It reveals a number of enduring features of Ryga's dramatic *oeuvre*: a strong social consciousness arising from his Marxist convictions; sympathy for the outsider (often an Indian); and a style that combines naturalistic and non-naturalistic conventions. Like Edward Albee's *Zoo Story*, which influenced it, *Indian* derives its power from the way Ryga invests a casual encounter with unexpected violence and menace.

The Ecstasy of Rita Joe is based on an actual incident, reported in a Vancouver newspaper, about the murder of an Indian girl whose body was found in a Vancouver slum rooming house. Foreshadowed in the play's opening scene, the murder of Rita Joe becomes a searing image of the destruction by an insensitive and brutal white society of the values of British Columbia Indians. The central theatrical convention controlling the fluidity of the play's development is the trial of Rita Joe; the audience (the jury) in a theatre (the courtroom) watches as the sensitive but unbending Magistrate questions Rita Joe, ultimately finding her guilty of the crimes—assault, shoplifting, vagrancy, and prostitution—with which she has been charged. But by the play's conclusion Ryga has skilfully led the audience to question the morality of the legal system that condemns Rita Joe. Her 'passion' (she is seduced, initiated into prostitution, alcoholism, and drug abuse, and eventually gang-raped and murdered) is followed by the 'ecstasy' of sainthood. The play in some ways resembles the morality play *Everyman*: Rita Joe has been given eight hours to find people who know her and will testify to her character; when she turns to her lover, to her father, to the Priest, and to the Teacher, they either will not or cannot help her. Rita Joe's passive father offers the parable of the caterpillar's metamorphosis into a dragon fly and its flight into the sun. Though beautiful, this is irrelevant to Rita Joe's suffering—and, by extension, to the suffering of her people.

'*The Ecstasy of Rita Joe*,' writes Christopher Innes, 'marked the birth of modern Canadian drama'; he argues that Ryga invented a new dramaturgy in which he could give theatrical shape and definition to stream-of-consciousness techniques that were traditionally the preserve of the novelist and poet. *Rita Joe* is not a 'memory play'; rather it is a sustained montage divorced from causality and a regular time-sequence. Ryga's dramaturgy was complemented in the original production by the use of a number of discrete acting areas, identified by carefully controlled lighting effects. The Singer of the play is a Brechtian borrowing meant at once to distance the action and to emphasize the inevitability of Rita Joe's fate. And the play owes much to the poetic language given the Indians (as opposed to the stripped functional language of white society and the law). 'A train whistle is white, with black lines. . . .' Rita Joe says. 'A sad woman is a room with the curtains shut.'

The Vancouver première of *The Ecstasy of Rita Joe* featured some of Canada's finest actors. Frances Hyland played Rita Joe, with August Schellenberg as Jamie Paul. The Indian actor Chief Dan George brought a special authority to his portrayal of Rita Joe's father. Ann Mortifee was the Singer; George Bloomfield directed. The quality of production, together with the originality of Ryga's dramaturgy and the extraordinary relevance of his subject, was influential in demonstrating that a native and professional theatre was viable in Canada.

None of Ryga's subsequent plays have scored the same critical and popular success as *The Ecstasy of Rita Joe*. *Grass and Wild Strawberries*, produced by the Vancouver Playhouse in 1969, uses rock music, dance, and film projections to comment on the conflict between a bourgeois society and the new alternate culture of the 1960s. *Captives of the Faceless Drummer* (1971) is more overtly political, depicting a confrontation between a revolutionary leader and a kidnapped diplomat. Commissioned by the Vancouver Playhouse, the play has many analogies to the 1970 October Crisis (when a Quebec Cabinet minister was kidnapped and assassinated by the FLQ) and the board of the Playhouse refused to produce it; as a result the Vancouver Art Gallery presented the première in April 1971. *Sunrise on Sarah* (1973), produced by the Banff School of Fine Arts in 1972, represents the various stages in a middle-class woman's life as she is interviewed by the man, an artist-psychiatrist. Sarah's search for values is a theme given enormous amplification in *Paracelsus*, published in 1974, but not produced until 1987 (by the Vancouver Playhouse). Here Ryga selects the story of the sixteenth-century physician and alchemist to show how a history play might have relevance for contemporary audiences and to express dissatisfaction with the contemporary 'lack of really heroic standards'. Paracelsus represents the revolutionary spirit, or outsider, who champions a new spirit of enquiry and is martyred by the forces of reaction. (He has obvious affinities with Dr Norman Bethune and with Che Guevara.) But Ryga's attempt to make Paracelsus' story relevant by having two doctors in a present-day hospital debate the inadequacies of twentieth-century medical practice ('I'm a business man,' argues one of these doctors, 'and screw your Schweitzers and Bethunes!') is contrived, and unrelated to the main concerns of the play. The play's greatest weakness, however, is its verse. 'No play should be written in verse for which prose is *dramatically* adequate,' T.S. Eliot once wrote. The inadequacy of Ryga's verse is most apparent in its laboured metaphors and similes. Paracelsus speaks of the wisdom he has gained as 'but a flicker / Of a candle in the centre of a vast, / Enshrouded sea . . . .' To a priest he declaims, 'You bore me, as a nightingale in time / Bores a drowsy man.' 'Nay, nay . . . do not blanch,' he tells his companion, 'as a widow in the presence of a stallion.'

The protagonists of several of Ryga's plays are working-class people (prospectors, immigrants) cast in a larger-than-life mould that reflects the 'heroic standards' Ryga prizes. *A Letter to My Son* is typical of these plays. Commissioned and first produced by Kam Theatre Lab, Thunder Bay, Ontario, in October 1981, it grew out of a screenplay written by Ryga for 'Newcomers', a CBC television series on immigration to Canada. Ryga's stage directions call for two levels: one where the protagonist of the play, Old Lepa, a Ukrainian immigrant, 'encounters his memories'; the other where he spars with Nancy, a social worker who is trying to get some form of documentation from Lepa so that he may obtain an old-age pension. *A Letter to My Son* is a slow-paced elegiac evening of reminiscence, deficient in theatricality and lacking in a single dominant dramatic focus. Its resolution, where Old Lepa is reconciled with Nancy, is uncharacteristically saccharine and pat.

But if the quality of Ryga's work is uneven, his dedication to his craft, and his unrelenting commitment to the value of theatre as a vital social force, are impressive. Urging the importance of the past, Ryga has attempted to identify—and to create—the archetypes and context of a Canadian mythology. And his plays are valued as additions to a literature that is distressingly apolitical. In expressing his passion for reform, Ryga has shown how the writer can become *engagé* without succumbing to narrow ideology.

While the Stratford Festival's production of James Reaney's *Colours in the Dark* in July 1967, and its earlier workshop production of John Herbert's *Fortune and Men's Eyes*, had suggested at least the possibility of fruitful collaboration between the Festival and Canada's playwrights, Stratford gave a sign that it was not inclined to make a commitment to new Canadian work when *Fortune* eventually premièred in the United States. Similarly, the Vancouver Playhouse's encouragement of George Ryga in 1967 pointed to opportunities for the country's regional theatres to support the development of Canadian drama, but unfortunately the record of the regional theatres in this regard is not impressive.

Established in the 1960s with substantial financial support from federal, provincial, and municipal governments, the regional theatres were intended to stimulate the professional development of Canadian theatre in all its aspects, including the drama. The Canada Council urged that the first of the new regional theatres—the Manitoba Theatre Centre (1958)—should be the prototype for other regional theatres because of its perceived commitment to its immediate community and the province, and because of its stated aim to present Canadian plays. But the building of spacious and well-equipped theatres (with high operating costs) does not guarantee the creation of a significant indigenous drama; in fact the necessity to fill large capacity halls— Vancouver's Playhouse Theatre seats 647, the Shoctor at Edmonton's Citadel Theatre 685, the Bluma Appel at Toronto's CentreStage 894, the Beaverbrook at Theatre New Brunswick 763—may hinder it. A 1971 study showed that of 108 plays produced by seven regional theatres between 1965 and 1971, only nineteen were Canadian. To respond to this neglect the Canada Council, in the summer of 1971, organized a conference in the Gaspé, Quebec, which issued the Gaspé Manifesto. The manifesto recommended that 'the grant-giving agencies make it a policy that the theatres they support become Canadian in content [and] that such theatres be required to achieve a fifty-percent Canadian content (one play in two) no later than January 1973.' The Council endorsed, but refused to enforce, the recommendation, and its hope that theatres would voluntarily Canadianize their repertoire was not realized. For example, the 1976 season of the Manitoba Theatre Centre was dominated by the plays of Shakespeare, Coward, Shaffer, Steinbeck, Albee, Beckett, and Lerner. Toronto's St Lawrence Centre did not offer a single Canadian play in 1976—its *pièce-de-résistance* was *You're a Good Man, Charlie Brown*.

To be sure, there were honourable exceptions to the general neglect of Canadian plays by the regional theatres. Since its inaugural season in 1969–70, the Centaur—Montreal's major English-language theatre—has produced some fifty Canadian works, several by David Fennario, the playwright who has been most closely identified with it. In Regina the Globe Theatre (founded in 1966) has remained firmly rooted in its community; Rex Deverell, the Globe's long-time playwright-in-residence has contributed many plays based on local and regional concerns—among them, *Medicare!* (produced in 1980) about the 1960 Saskatchewan doctors' strike, and *Black Powder* (produced in 1981) to commemorate the thirtieth anniversary of the Estevan coal mine riots. And the mandate of Quebec's Festival Lennoxville was to produce *only* Canadian plays, a policy it maintained during its ten-year existence (1972–82), just as Ontario's Blyth Festival has upheld a commitment to Canadian plays since its inception in 1975.

Nevertheless, despite the hopes generated in 1967 and the expectations of the Canada Council, the main thrust of the country's major professional theatres throughout the sixties and seventies was to sustain a theatrical culture heavily dependent upon imported plays. In addition, some of these theatres were still looking abroad—particularly to the United Kingdom—for artistic directors: the Citadel brought in Peter Coe and Gordon McDougall in 1978 and 1984, and only federal government intervention prevented the appointment of John Dexter as Stratford's artistic director during the controversy that followed

Robin Phillips' resignation in 1980. But whether the country's festival and regional theatres were controlled by foreign or Canadian artistic directors scarcely seemed to matter. Until the 1980s Canadian plays achieved only a token presence in their repertoires. Developments in alternate theatre, however, offered playwrights new encouragement.

THE ALTERNATE THEATRE

The alternate theatre in Canada emerged in the 1960s from various aesthetic, cultural, and political influences. Deliberately opposing established values and conventions, alternate theatre was an international phenomenon that manifested itself in diverse ways—from rudimentary street theatre, to iconoclastic New York repertory ensembles like Julian Beck's Living Theatre, to the 1967 Broadway rock musical, *Hair*. An anti-Vietnam War show, *Hair* also provocatively celebrated sexual promiscuity, drugs, communes, and political protest. Ironically it played (in 1970) at the staid Royal Alexandra Theatre, while other anti-establishment successes in Toronto appeared in more appropriate venues—*Dionysus in '69* at Studio Lab Theatre in 1970, and *Chicago '70* at Toronto Workshop Productions, also in 1970. Another American play, Rochelle Owens' *Futz*—about a man sexually obsessed with a pig—ran at Toronto's Theatre Passe Muraille in 1969.

But the development of a distinctively Canadian alternate theatre in which Canadian writers could be fully involved was prompted more by a changing political climate at home and a groundswell of interest in Canadian history, culture, and institutions than by American influences. Spurred by celebrations such as the Festival of Underground Theatre held in Toronto in 1970, and funding assistance from two federal work programs—the Local Initiatives Program and Opportunities for Youth—alternate theatre companies multiplied across the country: Vancouver's New Play Centre (founded 1970) and Tamahnous Theatre (1971); Calgary's Alberta Theatre Projects (1972); Edmonton's Theatre 3 (1970) and Theatre Network (1975); Saskatoon's 25th Street Theatre (1971); Halifax's Pier One (1971); Newfoundland's Mummers Troupe (1972) and Codco (1973); and several in Toronto, including Theatre Passe Muraille (1968), Factory Theatre Lab (1970), Tarragon Theatre (1971), and Toronto Free Theatre (1972).

The forerunner of these theatres was Toronto Workshop Productions, founded by George Luscombe in 1959. Luscombe spent five years working in England with Joan Littlewood's famous Theatre Workshop, and this experience shaped his direction of TWP, Canada's first alternate theatre. Politically motivated (with a decidedly left-wing focus), Luscombe's work emphasized a collective approach to theatrical production (the playwright was simply one collaborator among many equal collaborators) and a preference for theatrical imagination and skills rather than textual sophistication. This approach led to many successful productions; *Hey Rube!*, a circus play, first produced in 1961, was one of TWP's early achievements. But despite Luscombe's long and iconoclastic tenure at TWP (he stepped down from the artistic directorship in 1986), he never achieved the influence in the Canadian alternate theatre movement that might have been expected from his early enterprise, perhaps because of his international rather than national perspective on culture and politics.

Other alternate theatres, however, deliberately adopted a specifically Canadian character. Theatre Passe Muraille, founded by Jim Garrard, was certainly influenced in its beginnings by the aesthetics of international theatre, particularly the theories of French actor and director Antonin Artaud: the name—theatre without walls—represented a rejection of traditional concepts of theatrical space in order to allow the actors to relate more closely to their audience and to give greater emphasis to theatre as experience or event. (TPM's theatre is a flexible space where seating varies, according to the kind of production, from 200 to 400.) However, when Paul Thompson became artistic director in 1971 he added a nationalistic dimension to Garrard's Artaudian views. Thompson had considerable knowledge of European theatre theory and practice—he had written a University of Toronto M.A. thesis on Artaud, and had studied with the innovative French director Roger Planchon at the Théâtre de la Cité in Villeurbanne, near Lyon—but he determined to apply the techniques he acquired in Europe to a theatrical endeavour that would address identifiable Canadian social and political issues (which he had been unable to do during the two years he spent at the Stratford Festival after returning from France). This social and political awareness expressed through collective creation is the trademark of TPM's work. The collectives were, and are, developed by the actors. Alternate theatre seeks to demythologize the dramatist, the director, and even the individual actor, and although too many collectives of the 1970s produced merely a string of vignettes, the final collective product under a director as gifted as Thompson can convey a rare sense of authenticity—as happened, for example, with TPM's *The Farm Show*. In the summer of 1972 Thompson and his actors lived in the farming community of Clinton, Ontario, where they created a series of sketches, monologues, songs, and dramatized metaphors and images that they first performed in a Clinton barn. What is striking about the play (or 'show', as the actors preferred to call it) is the poetic valorization given to local language when it is linked to Thompson's distinctive theatricality—which, paradoxically, is rooted in documentary detail and particularized props. Although largely pastoral in character, *The Farm Show* proved immensely appealing to urban and rural audiences alike. With this production it was clear that TPM under Thompson had moved away from the internationalism represented by its earlier production of *Futz* to indigenous material that would enable the company to incorporate local speech, customs, and traditions into plays that attempted to create a Canadian mythology and retell Canada's history.

Not all the collectives were rural in character. In fact, TPM's most successful play in box-office terms was its 1975 production, *I Love You, Baby Blue*, a provocative exploration of sexual mores in contemporary Toronto. The best known of TPM's historical collectives— revisionist history with a vengeance—was *1837; The Farmers' Revolt*, written with Rick Salutin and produced in 1973.

Theatre Passe Muraille provided an example—and, often, direct help—to other such companies across Canada. In Newfoundland the Mummers Troupe, under founder Chris Brookes, adopted the collective approach while adding a tough political agitprop style. *Gros Mourn*, produced in 1973, dramatized the plight of a community forced to relocate when a national park was being created; *They Club Seals, Don't They?*, produced in 1978, was a hard-hitting defence of the sealing industry. In Saskatchewan, 25th Street Theatre scored a success in Saskatoon in 1977, and subsequently on a national tour and on television, with *Paper Wheat*, a collective revue about prairie farming. British Columbia's numerous alternate theatres (it has been estimated that prior to 1975 there were some forty of them in Vancouver alone) did not avoid the socio-political, but tended to reflect the interests of west-coast American (particularly Californian) culture; this resulted in plays about drugs, dreams, fantasies, and various psychological conditions. Therapeutic plays like *Deep Thought* and *Vertical Dreams* (produced in 1977 and 1979 respectively) were prominent at Tamahnous Theatre.

While several of Canada's alternate theatres specialized in collective creations and documentaries (or docu-dramas), in which text was not a pre-eminent consideration, other alternates offered direct encouragement and opportunities to the Canadian playwright. However, as a member of a collective, the playwright does not retain the traditional authority over text, nor—if the purpose of a collective creation is to advocate a particular social or political position—have the freedom to allow the play to take imaginative directions that might be artistically valid, but politically inappropriate. It is also true that if a collective—or, indeed, any advocacy play—is to make its point unequivocally it cannot dally with complexity of theme or subtlety of characterization. These restrictions mean that the collective will attract only a relatively small number of playwrights. Even Rick Salutin, who has worked closely with Theatre Passe Muraille, has spoken of collectives as 'predictable', and lacking 'intricacy'. In a 1982 interview he expressed doubts about their future: 'It's hard to know where collectives can go. I would say that in the last few years there haven't been many serious attempts to develop the form, to do something more mature with it.'

Among the alternate theatres that nurtured Canadian playwrights was Toronto Free Theatre (admission was literally free until 1974), where Carol Bolt's *Gabe* and *Red Emma* were first presented (in 1973 and 1974 respectively), and where one of Erika Ritter's earliest plays, *The Splits*, received its première in 1978. Toronto Free has also produced plays by Anne Chislett, David Fennario, George Walker, and other leading playwrights, but even stronger support for the playwright has come from two other Toronto alternates: Factory Theatre Lab and Tarragon Theatre.

Ken Gass called his Factory Theatre Lab 'The Home of the Canadian Playwright'; in his eight seasons as artistic director he produced, in addition to work-in-progress and experimental pieces, a number of significant new plays that included David Freeman's *Creeps* and *Battering Ram*, Larry Fineberg's *Death* and *Stonehenge Trilogy*, several plays by George Walker, Herschel Hardin's *Esker Mike and his*

Wife, Agiluk, and plays by Hrant Alianak, Louis del Grande, Michael Hollingsworth, John Palmer, Bryan Wade, and several by Gass himself.

The Tarragon Theatre, founded by Bill Glassco, made its reputation by discovering new Canadian playwrights and producing their work with an imaginative professionalism in a small theatre that originally seated only 180. Although Tarragon's mandate did not exclude the production of non-Canadian plays, in its first few seasons it produced David French's *Leaving Home* and *Of the Fields, Lately*; James Reaney's Donnelly trilogy; Michel Tremblay's *Hosanna* and *Forever Yours, Marie-Lou* (both in English); and David Freeman's *Creeps* and *Battering Ram*. Of the approximately one hundred plays produced to date by Tarragon, about three-quarters have been Canadian, and over half of these have been premières—a remarkable testament to the theatre's commitment to the Canadian playwright. It is not simply a matter of *receiving* scripts (though some 400–500 unsolicited scripts are annually assessed at Tarragon), it is also a matter of *developing* scripts—through such projects as the playwright-in-residence program and the Six Playwrights Unit, established in 1982 by Urjo Kareda, Bill Glassco's successor as Tarragon's artistic director.

THREE ALTERNATE PLAYWRIGHTS:
DAVID FREEMAN, GEORGE WALKER, DAVID FRENCH

Of the dozens of Canadian playwrights whose careers began in the alternate theatres in the 1970s, three stand out for the quality and durability of their work: David Freeman and George Walker at Factory Theatre Lab, and David French at Tarragon.

Born with cerebral palsy, David Freeman attended a school for the handicapped in Toronto before enrolling at McMaster University and graduating with a degree in political science in 1971. At the suggestion of Bill Glassco, he developed an article about sheltered workshops he had written for *Maclean's* in 1964 into a play. The production of *Creeps* at Factory Theatre Lab in February 1971 was an immediate critical and box-office success, so much so that Glassco chose it to open his new Tarragon Theatre in October 1971. Urjo Kareda described it as 'unique and absorbing . . . glorious and defiant' (*Toronto Star*, 6 October 1971).

Creeps is a long one-act play set in the men's washroom of a sheltered workshop. Five residents, all afflicted with cerebral palsy, retreat to the washroom from their mindless workshop jobs (folding boxes, sanding blocks) to argue about their lot and to give vent to the frustrations they all experience. The thin plot line turns on the efforts of Tom, a would-be painter, to persuade Jim, who has potential as a writer, to leave the false security of the workshop and live independently. Jim lacks the courage, and at the play's end Tom departs alone as the mad Thelma—who has been raped by another of the characters—closes the play with the chilling cry that has been heard throughout the action: 'I need a priest! Get me a priest! Someone get me a priest!'

Freeman's handling of Thelma (who is heard but never seen) is problematical; if she is indeed now mentally as well as physically handicapped her continuing presence in the workshop seems improbable. And the characters of Carson and Saunders—workshop officials—are merely stereotyped authority figures. Yet the strengths of the play are abundant. Each of the main characters is carefully delineated, and Freeman provides precise directions for their distinct physical movements. The particular attitude of each character to his situation is equally well crafted, often by language and behaviour that is uncomfortably crude and scatological, yet—as in *Fortune and Men's Eyes*—entirely appropriate to the situation. A tremendous challenge to the actors performing the handicapped characters, *Creeps* is both visually disturbing and theatrically vibrant. The three 'hallucinatory interruptions' presenting 'a nightmare vision of organized charity, all rowdy, romping do-gooders and an obscenely grinning Miss Cerebral Palsy' (Urjo Kareda's apt description) have struck some critics as at best irrelevant, at worst gratuitously offensive; but if they offend they do so for good reason—they offer vivid and memorable images of the patronizing attitude of charitable organizations that handicapped people find so objectionable. *Creeps* is hardly a balanced analysis of society's treatment of victims of cerebral palsy, but it movingly captures the sense of helplessness felt by Tom and his fellow sufferers: 'It's like I'm at the bottom of a grave yelling "I'm alive! I'm alive!" But they don't hear me. They just keep shovelling in the dirt.'

Winner of the first Chalmers Award (for the outstanding play produced in the Toronto area) and of a New York Critics Drama Desk award, *Creeps* remains Freeman's best play. *Battering Ram* (produced at Factory Theatre Lab in April 1972), in which a middle-aged woman and her daughter prey upon a cripple and are, in turn, preyed upon by him, and *You're Gonna Be Alright, Jamie Boy* (first produced by the Tarragon Theatre in January 1974), about a family's addiction to alcohol and television, are well-written plays, but they lack the power that emanates from the scabrous world of *Creeps*. Freeman's latest play, *Flytrap*, first produced in 1976, is a disappointing domestic drama (husband, wife, and young male tenant), that is derivative (particularly of Albee and Pinter) and unengaging.

A writer of plays as provocative as *Creeps* and *Jamie Boy* could never have received encouragement from the large middle-class regional theatres in the early 1970s. Only the existence of the alternates gave Freeman his opportunity. Similarly Factory Theatre Lab provided a congenial home for the idiosyncratic talents of George F. Walker, a native of Toronto's east end. Ten of Walker's plays have premièred at the Factory (including the first seven he wrote), and he was the theatre's playwright-in-residence from 1971 to 1976 and artistic director for 1978–9. His plays have also been produced at Tarragon Theatre, Toronto Free Theatre, CentreStage (Toronto), and abroad.

Three of Walker's early plays—*Bagdad Saloon*, *Beyond Mozambique*, and *Ramona and the White Slaves*—have been published in *Three Plays by George Walker* (1978). *Beyond Mozambique*, first produced at the Factory Theatre Lab in May 1974, is representative of the subject matter and style of these early plays. The bizarre array of characters includes a porn-movie star, a mad ex-Nazi doctor, the doctor's wife (who thinks she is one of Chekhov's three sisters), a junkie priest, and an RCMP corporal, all gathered in a dilapidated house in an African jungle. The play is part surreal, part melodrama; its point of view is absurdist (too self-consciously so); and it is deliberately imitative of the cartoon (*Bagdad Saloon* is sub-titled 'A Cartoon') and the B-movie. In *Beyond Mozambique*, as in many of his plays, Walker's frenzied imagination concerns itself with the nature of evil; Rocco, the doctor, steeped in corruption, declares his baseness to be his strength.

A more thoroughly developed exploration of this subject gave Walker his first major success, *Zastrozzi: the Master of Discipline*, which premièred at Toronto Free Theatre in November 1977. *Zastrozzi* fuses the elements that characterize Walker's dramaturgy: high seriousness punctuated by low comedy, the deliberate mining of other genres (in this case film, gothic melodrama, and the revenge tragedy in particular), deadpan aphorisms that guy the sententious ('the best advice is that of the best advised'), literary parody, bold theatricality, and a quirky and enduring interest in metaphysical questions that are continually being undercut by a cynical pragmatism. Although New York critics were not greatly impressed with *Zastrozzi* when it was produced there in 1982—'a trying 90-minute fable' that 'refuses to rise above pedantry' was Frank Rich's judgement in the *New York Times* (18 January 1982)—the play takes risks that more often than not pay off. The plot turns on the attempts of master-criminal Zastrozzi to track down his mother's murderer, but *Zastrozzi* is more than a revenge play. The central conflict between the monstrous Zastrozzi and the values of art and liberalism poses moral conundrums that linger long after the play's sometimes laboured dialogue and shallow philosophizing have been forgotten.

Another collection of Walker's plays, *The Power Plays*, was published in 1984. Unified by their central character, Tyrone M. Power, the three comic murder/mystery plays in the collection—*Gossip*, *Filthy Rich*, and *The Art of War*—form a natural trilogy, although they do not achieve the coherence of David French's Mercer trilogy or James Reaney's Donnellys trilogy because *The Art of War* is on an altogether higher plane of seriousness and intelligence (posing troublesome questions again about the value of 'liberalism' in the face of autocratic power) than either *Gossip* or *Filthy Rich*. The only recognizable coherence in the Power plays comes from Power himself. One of the most intriguing characters in recent Canadian drama, Power is an unsuccessful journalist, failed novelist, and reluctant private detective who bungles his way through life in traditional anti-hero fashion. He looks the part ('middle-aged and balding. Walrus mustache. Thick-rimmed glasses. A bit overweight') and acts the part ('Why can't we do anything properly. It's so goddam depressing'). Cynical, frequently serious, he is a moralist who seeks out truth and justice with dedication but inefficiency. His ultimate triumphs in solving murder cases in *Gossip* and *Filthy Rich* are not matched in *The Art of War*, where political manipulation and corruption overcome his good intentions. Walker creates a rich array of characters in

The Power Plays—the portrait of John Hackman, militaristic adviser to the Minister of Culture in *The Art of War* is striking—but Power remains the principal focus.

Walker has also written a rock musical, *Rumours of our Death*, which he successfully directed himself (he has directed much of his own work) at Factory Theatre Lab in 1980. His more recent work has been somewhat repetitive: *Theatre of the Film Noir* (Factory Theatre Lab, 1981) draws on B-movies again; *Science and Madness* (Tarragon Theatre, 1982) is another portrait of evil (this time of a Frankenstein-like figure); and *Criminals in Love* (at Factory Theatre, the new name adopted by Factory Theatre Lab in 1984) is a variation on the criminality/morality theme of earlier plays. *Better Living*, a drama of family politics, was unsuccessful in its 1986 production at Toronto's CentreStage, where it seemed ill-suited both to the stage and to the audience of this large civic theatre. Nonetheless George Walker rarely fails to stimulate and to amuse.

David French also got his start at a Toronto alternate theatre, the Tarragon. Born in 1939 in Coley's Point, Newfoundland, French moved with his family to Toronto in 1945. During the 1960s he wrote dramas for CBC television before turning to stage plays. His first full-length play, *Leaving Home*, which premièred at Tarragon in May 1972 under the direction of Bill Glassco, drew on memories of his Newfoundland background and the difficulties his family experienced in adjusting to Toronto. The play dramatizes the conflict between Jacob Mercer and his son Ben. This archetypal father-son clash suggests also a clash between older heroic values (Newfoundland) and the mores of an urbanized society (Toronto). In the father's remembrance of Newfoundland—back home—men were stronger, women finer, and drinking sprees epic. The title of the play encapsulates the complex weave of the plot. Ben leaves home for Western Canada to escape his bull-headed, intolerant father; Kathy Jackson wants to marry Billy Mercer (Ben's brother) to escape the home represented by her brash, domineering mother, Minnie. Even Ben's parents, Jacob and Mary, are brought to the realization that Jacob must somehow abandon his home—Newfoundland—if he is to make peace with his family. A powerful blend of painful laceration and comedy (the comedy represented especially by an undertaker who never utters a word), *Leaving Home* is on one level a purely naturalistic play; but French enriches it, and his other plays, with a heightened—poetic—speech that gives his work symbolic reach.

The Mercer family reappears in French's second full-length play, *Of the Fields, Lately*, which premièred at Tarragon in September 1973, again directed by Glassco. It is two years later and Ben has returned home for his aunt's funeral. Whereas the action of *Leaving Home* had been framed by preparations for a wedding, the action of this second Mercer play is framed by the aunt's death and the imminent death of Jacob, who has suffered a heart attack. The inevitability of Jacob's death—suggested in the flashback scene that opens the play— lends *Of the Fields* a moving elegiac tone as Jacob, his stubbornness softened by intimations of his own mortality, grows closer to his wife, Mary, and reaches out tentatively to Ben. At the end of the play Ben leaves home again—not to save himself, but to save his father. When we learn from the epilogue (reminiscent of those in *The Glass Menagerie* and *Death of a Salesman*) that the death of the father has finally set Ben free, we realize how sensitively French has recreated the Oedipal conflict of father and son within a Canadian family.

French returned to the Mercer family more than ten years later with *Salt-Water Moon*, also directed by Bill Glassco when it opened at Tarragon in October 1984. The events of the two-character play take place in 1926 in Coley's Point and dramatize the courtship of Jacob Mercer and his future wife, Mary. While the play has sufficient inner cohesion and meaning to stand in its own right, it acquires added richness and reverberations from its association with the other plays of the Mercer trilogy. When we learn in *Salt-Water Moon* that Jacob's impoverished father had been humiliated by the father of Jerome McKenzie, to whom Mary is engaged, we understand Jacob's later intractability and independence of character. Because the outcome of Jacob's courtship of Mary is never in doubt, it is not the courtship but its process that is beguiling, one of changing relationships that also reflects the process of change in Newfoundland—the struggle of a proud and independent people to come to terms with new social and cultural realities. In language that ranges from the symbolic (much of it is drawn from astronomy), to the lyric ('the sun shining, the breeze making t'umbprints on the blue water') to the earthy ('See how straight Tom sits in the saddle, Mary. You'd swear he had an oar up his arse'), French has written a love story that is also an allegory about a couple's and a nation's passage from innocence to experience. The precise conception and delicate execution of *Salt-Water Moon* make it French's most satisfying play to date.

One Crack Out (about Toronto's criminal underworld) and *The Riddle of the World* (about ways of coping with breakdowns in human relationships), which premièred at Tarragon in 1975 and 1981 respectively, are not among French's best works, but *Jitters*, directed by Bill Glassco at Tarragon in February 1979 and frequently revived, deserved its enormous box-office and critical success. This play explores the various crises that erupt as a company rehearses a new play hoping that a famous New York critic will attend the première. Central to the play's ironies is the struggle of Canadian theatre to liberate itself from foreign theatrical dominance while needing to seek approval from New York or London. In *Jitters* French shows a fully professional command of craftsmanship in his handling of the play-within-a-play; the dialogue is sparkling and genuinely witty; the depth of the characterizations makes it a comedy rather than a mere farce or theatrical romp.

With the Mercer trilogy and *Jitters* David French has laid claim to being Canada's most accomplished playwright in English—accomplished in his command of structure, characterization, and dialogue. Unlike Sean O'Casey—to whom he has been compared—French is the dramatist of the quotidian, finding tragedy and comedy in everyday lives without the background of revolution and civil war that O'Casey draws upon. But he has O'Casey's ear for the poetry of colloquial speech and O'Casey's ability to deepen pathos by tempering it with the comic. Like Chekhov—whom he admires and whose work he has translated (*The Seagull*, produced at Tarragon in 1977)—his work is nostalgic, often bitter-sweet. But regardless of influences or resemblances, French's work represents a distinctively Canadian comment on the human condition.

REGIONALISM

While Toronto undoubtedly established itself as the centre of English-Canadian theatrical activity in the 1970s, a number of important playwrights developed allegiances to, and frequently wrote plays about, other regions of the country. In an important essay published in volume 85 (1980) of *Canadian Literature* Diane Bessai argues that regionalism should not be regarded as 'narrow, limited, parochial, backward, out-dated or isolationist'. Rather it is 'rooted, indigenous, shaped by a specific social, cultural and physical milieu'. In this sense regionalism has a lengthy tradition in Canadian drama. There is evidence of it in the nineteenth century (Maritime political satires, for instance) as well as in the plays of Merrill Denison, Herman Voaden, Gwen Pharis Ringwood, and later playwrights. Regionalism was particularly prominent in the 1970s, influencing playwrights as diverse as David Fennario, Michael Cook, Ken Mitchell, John Murrell, and Sharon Pollock, and shaping the repertoire both of major civic theatres and alternates.

Michael Cook, born in 1933 in England of Anglo-Irish parents, immigrated to Canada in 1965 and settled in St John's, Newfoundland. His first three stage plays—*Colour the Flesh the Colour of Dust*, first performed at Halifax's Neptune Theatre in 1972, *The Head, Guts and Sound Bone Dance*, first performed at the Arts and Culture Centre, St John's in 1973, and *Jacob's Wake*, first performed at Festival Lennoxville in 1975—constitute what has been termed Cook's Newfoundland trilogy, plays bound together not by common characters or a common theme but by the spirit and way of life of Newfoundland.

Colour the Flesh the Colour of Dust is a Brechtian 'epic' play about the Anglo-French struggle for control of St John's in 1762, while *The Head, Guts and Sound Bone Dance*, perhaps Cook's best play, has a contemporary setting and offers an unflinching portrayal of Newfoundland life. It invites comparison with Synge's *Riders to the Sea*, but it is far more particularized and more brutal in its characterization. Central to the play is eighty-year-old Skipper Pete, who embodies Cook's belief that the older generations of Newfoundland's fishermen resembled the ancient Greeks in their waging of what Cook describes as 'a satanic struggle' to impose order upon experience rendered frequently chaotic by a blind and savage nature.' '. . . the sea's a big place,' says the Skipper. 'Now a man's a small place. You've got to have order. Decency. There 'as to be a way of doing things. A man's way. That's why we're here, isn't it? They's only we left.' The Skipper's failure to help the drowning boy at the end of Act 1 seems dramatically implausible; but Cook is trying to suggest that just as the death of Maurya's last son in *Riders to the Sea* could not have been prevented, so man's efforts against fate, as symbolized by the ever-present seas around Newfoundland, are futile. The play contains memorable scenes: the confrontation between the Skipper and his daughter; the savagely comic dinner scene; the drunken dance that gives the play its title; the scene when Absalom, Skipper Pete's retarded sixty-year-old son, enters with the drowned boy in his arms; and the stage business of cooking, drinking, and eating—carefully choreographed ritualistic gestures meant to create order out of an arbitrary existence.

Jacob's Wake also has memorable scenes, though the final one—in which we see the ghostly resurrection of the mad whaling skipper telling his unsavoury and corrupt family, 'ye has to steer into the starm and face up to what ye are'—is neither good theatre nor a convincing resolution of the play's tensions. An uneasy mixture of realism and symbolism, flaunting melodramatic situations and one-dimensional characters, *Jacob's Wake* is nevertheless a splendid failure, for despite evident weaknesses it is an intensely emotional play, uncovering stark truths about a family's and perhaps a culture's disintegration.

Cook's preoccupation with the history and people of Newfound-land is further reflected in one-act plays such as *Quiller* and *Therese's Creed* (performed as a double bill at Montreal's Centaur Theatre in 1977), several radio plays, and the history plays *The Gayden Chronicles* (about a British sailor hanged in St John's in 1812) and *On the Rim of the Curve* (about the annihilation of Newfoundland's aboriginal Beothuk Indians). In the history plays, as in nearly all of Cook's work, the canvas is sweeping, the characters many, the design bold. Where David French has settled for the relatively mundane conflicts of a Newfoundland/Toronto family, Michael Cook has sought out the heroic, almost cataclysmic aspects of Newfoundland life.

As Cook is firmly associated with Newfoundland, so David Fennario is identified with the city of Montreal. In her 1945 novel *Bonheur d'occasion* (*The Tin Flute*), Gabrielle Roy wrote movingly of the lives of the poor in Saint-Henri, Montreal, and of the tragic inability of its young people to break out of a vicious trap of poverty and family; thirty years later David Fennario began documenting in his plays the lives of the poor in Pointe-Saint-Charles, immediately south of Saint-Henri. His Marxist viewpoint highlights the economic and political exploitation of Montreal's poor—both French and English—and the difficulty for the two groups, divided by language and culture, to make common cause. The one-act *On the Job*, first produced in 1975 at the Centaur Theatre, Montreal (where many of Fennario's plays have premièred), is about a wildcat strike in the shipping room of a dress factory. The characters are sharply etched, the language memorable for its earthiness and humour. The two-act *Nothing to Lose*, produced in 1976, depicts a group of truckers with 'nothing to lose' who decide to strike. They are advised by a young playwright, Jerry Nines—a too-transparent *persona* for Fennario. This unfortunate tendency to introduce himself into a work manifests itself in *Toronto*, produced in 1978, in which Jerry Nines is now casting a play called *Nothing to Lose*. *Moving*, a 1983 play about Anglo-French relationships in Quebec, and *Joe Beef*, performed by Black Rock Theatre—a Pointe-Saint-Charles community theatre group—at McGill University in 1985, were not well received. *Joe Beef* (a series of Marxist sketches on Canadian history) is a remarkably strident attack on the Montreal establishment.

Fennario's best play is *Balconville*. First produced at the Centaur in January 1979, directed by Guy Sprung, *Balconville* is set in a run-down tenement building in Pointe-Saint-Charles and concerns three families—the Paquettes, the Williams, and the Regans. In their quarrels and fights young confront old, French confront English, and weak men confront enduring women. The smouldering tensions of a few hot summer days finally explode in a real fire that threatens to engulf the entire neighbourhood. In one of the few unsatisfactory moments of the play the characters face the audience at the end, the English asking, 'What are we going to do?' the French, 'Qu'est-ce qu'on va faire?' Although this Brechtian intrusion does not sit comfortably with the realism of the rest of the play, the question is pertinent and the answer clear: it is not a matter of resolving differences between French and English, but of dealing with the injustices of a class structure that allows exploitation of the poor (both French and English) by the rich and powerful.

Like Michael Cook, Fennario can sympathize with his characters without sentimentalizing them. The working-class people of Pointe-Saint-Charles (particularly the men) can be lazy, apathetic, and bigoted. The women—especially Irene, who actively supports the Pointe

Action Committee—have more fortitude and determination. That the characters end the play by asking a question—even if it is obviously rhetorical—rather than taking action points to their inability to organize effective opposition to common enemies, such as landlords and politicians. But what *Balconville* risks losing here as political propaganda, it gains in dramatic resonance. In recognizing and illuminating the human dimensions of a political situation he deplores, Fennario has convincingly captured the real complexity of the situation. Repairing a broken step in *Balconville*'s tenement is a major achievement; repairing the damage caused by social injustice, the play suggests, is impossible without fundamental changes of attitudes and priorities by the victims of the injustice.

Canada's first thoroughly bilingual play (about one-third of the dialogue is in French), *Balconville* was a worthy winner of the 1979 Chalmers Award, and in 1981 it toured England. Other regional playwrights have gained international recognition, although the play that has helped make Calgary playwright John Murrell prominent abroad has no regional associations. Since its première at the 1977 Guelph Spring Festival, *Memoir* has been performed in over twenty-five countries—including a three-year run in Paris—and has been translated into some fifteen languages. It depicts a day late in the life of the great French actress Sarah Bernhardt. To help her write her memoir, Bernhardt compels Pitou, her shy and self-deprecatory servant and amanuensis, to play people from her past while she recreates herself as several younger Bernhardts. The interweaving of the actual play and the plays-within-a play create rich theatrical and character effects—effects that have been enhanced by such powerful actresses as Siobhan McKenna (who created the role of Sarah) and Delphine Seyrig (who played it in Paris).

Murrell's association with Calgary includes periods as playwright-in-residence with Alberta Theatre Projects (1975–6) and as dramaturge at Theatre Calgary (1981–2). Alberta Theatre Projects premièred his *Waiting for the Parade* in 1977. This bitter-sweet play portrays the lives of five Calgary women during the Second World War. In twenty-four scenes Murrell explores the women's backgrounds and their relationships with their families and husbands. Particularly affecting is the plight of Catherine, who is drawn to a lover as she loses the memory of her soldier-husband overseas. But each character achieves a credible identity in facing personal dilemmas that both mirror and surpass the ordinary. Like *Memoir*, *Waiting for the Parade* has been extensively produced in Canada and abroad. Calgary is also the setting for much of Murrell's *Farther West*, directed in its 1982 Theatre Calgary première by Robin Phillips. In marked contrast to the introspective, elegiac mood of *Memoir* and *Waiting for the Parade*, *Farther West* is a graphically physical dramatization of the westward odyssey of a prostitute. Seen by some critics as unduly sensational— there are scenes of brutal violence and sexual degradation—the play nonetheless is a powerful exposure and indictment of the seamier aspects of nineteenth-century western Canadian society, as well as an exciting vehicle for the actress (Martha Henry in the original production) who plays the independently minded prostitute May Buchanan. Murrell's next major play, *New World*, a comedy of family reunion set on Vancouver Island, which draws on both Chekhov and Shakespeare (especially *The Tempest*) was co-produced in 1984 by the National Arts Centre and Toronto's CentreStage, again directed by Robin Phillips.

Sharon Pollock is another playwright identified with Calgary. Her regional interest, however, encompasses much of Western Canada, and the subject matter of her plays—most notably in *Blood Relations*—is not exclusively Canadian. After working in a variety of theatre jobs in New Brunswick in the 1960s, Pollock moved to Calgary where she began to establish herself as a playwright. Her early plays show a strong interest in political issues, particularly as reflected in Canadian historical events. *Walsh*, for example (produced at Theatre Calgary in 1973), criticizes the hypocrisy and cruelty of the government of John A. Macdonald in forcing Sioux chief Sitting Bull and his people out of Canada in 1881 (where they had sought refuge after the Battle of the Little Bighorn in 1876). The play focuses on the dilemma facing Major James Walsh of the North West Mounted Police who befriends Sitting Bull and yet must enforce the government's position. While interesting as documentary drama, *Walsh* is weakened by pedestrian characters and dialogue and an inadequate definition of Walsh's dilemma. His struggle between conscience and duty is too easily resolved, and the audience is left feeling somewhat indifferent to his anguish.

Pollock's interest in the human aspect of political morality arises again in *The Komagata Maru Incident*, which premièred at the Vancouver Playhouse in 1976. The issue in this play is racism, as practised by the Canadian government in 1914 when a boat-load of Sikh immigrants was refused entry in Vancouver. An immigration officer, William Hopkinson, staunchly supports the policy, even though his own mother is a native of the Punjab. Reconciling his heritage with his current values and responsibilities creates psychological tensions that Hopkinson is unable to cope with and that ultimately lead to his death. The difficulty for the reader and audience, however, is one of focus: if the purpose of *The Komagata Maru Incident* is to condemn a racist Canadian government, it is not served by diverting interest so insistently to Hopkinson. A similar difficulty is evident in Pollock's *One Tiger to a Hill*, a play (first produced at Edmonton's Citadel Theatre in 1980) based on a 1975 hostage incident at a New Westminster, B.C., penitentiary. As Robert Nunn has argued, the individual relationships in *One Tiger to a Hill* create a 'sexual triangle' that 'imposes the stock motivations of melodrama onto a play that apparently intended to say something about the inhumanity of the prison system. . . .'

Sharon Pollock found the right balance between issue-oriented drama and the drama of personal psychology with *Blood Relations*, which premièred at Edmonton's Theatre 3 in March 1980. Again using historical subject matter—this time the infamous and unsolved murders of Andrew and Abby Borden in Fall River, Massachusetts, in 1892—Pollock succeeds on many levels. Despite our knowledge that the murders have not been solved, *Blood Relations* grippingly recreates events surrounding the crime by using an intriguing play-within-a-play structure: ten years after the murders, the main suspect for the crime—the Bordens' daughter, Lizzie—plays the role of the family's maid while Lizzie's actress friend plays the role of Lizzie. Because the actress is obliged to put herself in Lizzie's position, she is better able—as is the audience—to appreciate and understand the circumstances that might well have driven Lizzie to kill her violent and insensitive father and her devious, self-serving stepmother. As interpreted by the actress, Lizzie is violent, stubborn, and sharp-tongued, but what gradually emerges is a portrait of a strong-willed woman—unmarried and with diminishing prospects of being able to support herself—trapped by the oppressive conventions of a society that give a woman in her position few opportunities for self-fulfilment. The death of her parents—and the inheritance that comes with it—give Lizzie the independence she might otherwise never have achieved. Thus, subtly and unobtrusively, Pollock advocates a feminist cause without compromising the moral complexity of the situation or the richness of structure and characterization in the play.

Subsequent plays by Pollock have not matched the achievement of *Blood Relations*. The volume in which it was first published, *Blood Relations and Other Plays* (1981)—winner of a Governor General's Award for Drama—also contains *One Tiger to a Hill* and *Generations* (produced in 1980 by Calgary's Alberta Theatre Projects). Robert Nunn has detected 'an almost Chekhovian approach' in *Generations*, an analogy that aptly describes its pace but not its quality, for this play of crumbling prairie farm life lacks the social and psychological depth of Pollock's earlier plays, let alone of Chekhov's. There is greater pace and urgency in *Whiskey Six*, a play about prohibition in the 1920s (first produced at Theatre Calgary in 1983), and the partly autobiographical *Doc*—about family discord—which again premièred at Theatre Calgary (in 1984) and won a 1986 Governor General's Award.

The regional playwright *par excellence* is Ken Mitchell. Born and raised in Moose Jaw, Saskatchewan, he draws on the Saskatchewan environment for much of his work. His protagonists reveal Mitchell's marked sympathy for strong nonconformist, even eccentric, characters. *The Medicine Line*, first produced in 1976, predates Sharon Pollock's treatment in *Walsh* of the relations between Major James Walsh and Sitting Bull, while *Davin: The Politician* depicts the life of the mercurial prairie politician Nicholas Flood Davin, including his affair with feminist Kate Simpson-Hayes. *Davin* was first produced in 1978, as was *The Shipbuilder*, a powerful story of a proud, independent Finnish homesteader who decides to build a ship on his farm, transport it to the Saskatchewan River, and sail it to his homeland. Pride and independence also characterize the protagonists of *Gabriel Dumont: The Plainsman*, which premièred at Saskatoon's 25th Street Theatre in 1985, and *Gone the Burning Sun*, which traces the life of Dr Norman Bethune, following him through medical school, marriage, the Spanish Civil War, to his death in China in 1939. In 1987 *Gone the*

Burning Sun toured China, with David Fox as Bethune, the role he created at the 1984 Guelph Spring Festival. Mitchell's interest in China was strengthened by a year in 1980–1 as visiting professor of English at the University of Nanking. He had already explored some features of Chinese politics and culture in *The Great Cultural Revolution*, a 1979 play dramatizing the plight of a playwright facing death because of his political views.

Mitchell is an extremely versatile playwright whose work ranges from the comedy of *Showdown at Sand Valley: A Western Entertainment*, a satire (first produced in 1977) that pits an American gunslinger against a Mountie in a small Saskatchewan town, to the tragic futility of *The Shipbuilder*. His 1975 *Cruel Tears* is a musical—created with the country and western group Humphrey and the Dumptrucks—based on Shakespeare's *Othello* that turns the story into a tale of love and rivalry among Saskatchewan truck drivers. Another musical, *Chautauqua Girl*, premièred in 1982. It is based on the life of Nola Erickson, wife of the manager of the Canadian Chautauqua (or tent shows) that toured the prairies in the 1920s and 1930s.

Mitchell's work, like that of other regional playwrights, demonstrates the validity of Diane Bessai's argument that regional drama need not be parochial or narrow. Mitchell is a man of wide reading and experience who elicits universal appeal from regional characters and history, and he writes as convincingly of international locales (Spain, China) as of Saskatchewan life.

NEW BEARINGS

Productions of plays by regional playwrights are not, of course, limited to particular regions of the country. Nor are they limited to particular kinds of theatres. A play like John Murrell's *Waiting for the Parade* might be seen anywhere in the country (or abroad), in small alternate theatres, large civic theatres, or amateur community theatres. Indeed, by the late 1970s the lines of demarcation between alternate and civic (or mainstream or regional) theatres were becoming blurred. In a 1979 article in the *Canadian Theatre Review* (no. 21) Ken Gass suggested that the term 'alternate' was already archaic. Tarragon's 1976–7 season, for example, did not differ greatly from the sort of repertoire to be found at the civic theatres. There were Canadian plays by Carol Bolt (*One Night Stand*) and Rudy Wiebe (*Far As the Eye Can See*), but Chekhov, Wedekind, and Strindberg were also presented. As if to emphasize the institutionalization of the alternate theatres, Urjo Kareda—the critic who had been so support-ive of the alternates—became literary manager at the Stratford Festival in 1975, and in the same year Bill Glassco (Tarragon's artistic director) was engaged to direct Robert Patrick's *Kennedy's Children* at the Festival, the alternate theatre's *bête noir*. Kareda returned to the alternates in 1982 when he succeeded Glassco as Tarragon's artistic director, but Glassco himself went on to take control of Toronto's main civic company, CentreStage, at the St Lawrence Centre. The extent of the broadening of the mandates of both alternate and civic theatres is graphically illustrated by two Toronto openings in May 1986: Rodgers and Hart's Broadway musical *Pal Joey* at Tarragon (directed by Vancouver alternate theatre stalwart Larry Lillo, and starring Stratford regular Martha Henry), and a new play by George Walker, *Better Living*, at CentreStage—a remarkable reversal of the normal artistic focus of these two companies. Meanwhile the Shaw Festival was venturing from its placid summer haven at Niagara-on-the-Lake into a Toronto winter season with provocative plays like François-Louis Tilly's *Delicatessen* (produced at Toronto Free Thea-tre in January 1984) and Wedekind's *Spring Awakening* (produced at the St Lawrence Centre in April 1986). To cap it all, it was announced in February 1987 that CentreStage will merge with Toronto Free Theatre, one of the city's earliest alternates, to form a new company, the goal of which, said Glassco and the Free's artistic director Guy Sprung, 'is to create a theatre which bridges the gap between the small "alternative" theatres which have fostered most of the new Canadian drama of the past twenty years, and the larger, more tradi-tional "regional" and festival theatres whose repertoires mainly consist of classics and contemporary plays from other countries.'

This broadening of mandates was beneficial, for it gave more oppor-tunities for bringing Canadian plays to a wider audience, and it provided new challenges for actors, dramaturges, directors, and designers at the alternates. The danger, however, was that if the alternate theatres were to compromise their original 'anti-establishment' mandates, there would be a significant gap in the Canadian theatrical spectrum.

However, this danger was nullified both by the existing alternates' continued, if not exclusive, emphasis on new and experimental work (in some cases in new performance spaces, such as Tarragon's Extra Space, opened in 1983) and by the emergence of a new generation of alternate theatres in the late 1970s and in the 1980s.

In Ottawa the Great Canadian Theatre Company was founded in 1975. Located in a small theatre in a former auto body shop, GCTC produces mostly socialist Canadian plays. Nova Scotia's Mulgrave Road Co-op Theatre, founded in 1977, is a collectively run touring company that creates plays reflecting the interests and concerns of its rural Nova Scotian audiences. In Toronto several small avant-garde companies are associated with the Toronto Theatre Centre: Buddies in Bad Times, A.K.A. Performance Interfaces, Necessary Angel Theatre Company, and Nightwood Theatre. According to artistic director Sky Gilbert (as quoted in *Canadian Theatre Review*, no. 38), Buddies in Bad Times, founded in 1979, aims to 'explore the relationship of the printed word to theatrical image in the belief that with the poet-playwright lies the future of Canadian theatre.' The company's identity, however, arises more from its productions of plays with a homosexual slant—*Cavafy* and *Pasolini/Pelosi*, for example. A.K.A. Performance Interfaces seeks to relate traditional theatre to video, film, electronic music, and dance. Toronto's Video Cabaret, under the direction of playwright Michael Hollingsworth, has a similar purpose. Richard Rose's Necessary Angel Theatre Company is best known for its production of John Krizanc's *Tamara*, first produced at the 1981 Toronto Theatre Festival and winner of five Dora Awards in that year. Set in the country home of Italian poet Gabriele d'Annunzio in 1927, *Tamara*, in Krizanc's words, is 'about art, politics, and the artist's responsibility.' The form of the play is highly unusual: it is designed to be performed not in a theatre but in a large house where multiple scenes are played simultaneously in different rooms. Thus audience members are free to shape the play through the scenes they choose to watch—in a sense, creating their own play. *Tamara* has proven to be an international hit, enjoying long runs in Mexico City and Los Angeles. Krizanc's *Prague*, which premièred at Tarragon in 1984, is a more conventional play, but it again explores the relation between art and politics. A theatre director in Prague wishes to stage a politically subversive play (which will destroy the

The 1984 Tarragon Theatre production of John Krizanc's *Prague*. From left to right: Richard Rose (director), Bruce Vavrina, Tanja Jacobs, Richard McMillan, Nancy Beatty. (Photo: Andrew Oxenham.)

company) to make amends for having once betrayed his father (to save the company). The plays within the play draw attention to the illusionary nature of drama; as metatheatre, *Prague* deconstructs and demystifies art's pretensions in a totalitarian society.

Nightwood Theatre was founded in 1979 by Cynthia Grant, Mary Vingoe, Maureen White, and Kim Renders as a collective interested in creating theatre that draws on literature, painting, and music. Their 1980 *Glazed Tempera*, for example, was inspired by the paintings of Alex Colville. In a short time, however, Nightwood became identified with feminist issues and many of its plays—such as Banuta Rubens' *Pope Joan*, produced in 1984—have a distinct feminist perspective. Nightwood was not the first of Canada's feminist theatres. Winnipeg's Nellie McClung Theatre opened in 1968, and the movement gathered strength in the late 1970s and 1980s, spurred by women's perception that they must be allowed to play a larger role in creating Canada's theatre. Statistics in a 1982 report prepared by Rina Fraticelli demonstrated that of 1,156 productions staged at 104 Canadian theatres between 1978 and 1981, only 10% of the plays were written by women, and only 13% of the directors were women; furthermore, only 11% of Canada's artistic directors were women. Among the companies seeking to redress this situation is Hecate's Players, founded in 1983 in Edmonton to promote readings of feminist texts in performance. And since 1982 Toronto's annual Five-Minute Feminist Cabaret has offered explicitly feminist work, though in the form of sketches rather than developed plays. If the number of women playwrights is still relatively small, it includes some distinguished names: Betty Lambert (*Jenny's Story*); Judith Thompson (*The Crackwalker, White Biting Dog*); Margaret Hollingsworth (*Ever Loving, Mother Country*); Joanna Glass (*Artichoke, Canadian Gothic, American Modern*); Cam Hubert (*Rites of Passage*); Erika Ritter (*Automatic Pilot*); Anne Chislett (*Quiet in the Land*); Beverley Simons (*Crabdance*); Carol Bolt (*Buffalo Jump, One Night Stand*); and Sharon Pollock.

Another area that has witnessed extraordinary growth in recent years is Canadian theatre for young people. The first professional company performing drama for young people, Holiday Theatre of Vancouver, was founded in 1953; there are now dozens of Canadian children's plays available, by playwrights as accomplished as Len

Peterson, James Reaney, Carol Bolt, Paddy Campbell, Rex Deverell, Eric Nicol, Dennis Foon, and John Lazarus. Adaptations of poems and novels have also worked well for young audiences: Theatre Passe Muraille's 1983 production of Dennis Lee's *Alligator Pie*; Mordecai Richler's *Jacob Two-Two Meets the Hooded Fang* at Toronto's Young People's Theatre in 1978; the Charlottetown Festival's annual presentation of *Anne of Green Gables*. Some sixty professional Canadian companies now regularly produce theatre for young people. Among the leading English-language ones are the Mermaid Theatre, Halifax (founded 1972); Young People's Theatre, Toronto (1966); the Globe Theatre, Regina (1966), with prolific playwright-in-residence Rex Deverell, who has written many children's plays; Green Thumb Theatre, Vancouver (1975); and Kaleidoscope Theatre, Victoria (1974).

Significant shifts in the content and style of theatre for young audiences have occurred in the last few years. Science fiction, adventure, myths and legends, and history still engage playwrights and young audiences, and some of the plays of the early 1970s—such as Carol Bolt's musical, *Cyclone Jack*, about the Indian marathon runner Tom Longboat, and Len Peterson's *Billy Bishop and the Red Baron*—would bear revival. A growing awareness of the sophistication of young people has led, however, to far more plays dealing directly with issues pertinent to today's youth. In 1981 at Young People's Theatre artistic director Peter Moss staged John and Joan Lazarus' *Dreaming and Duelling*, a frank exploration of teenage sexual conflict. But the most adventurous and stimulating work of this kind has been at Green Thumb Theatre, where co-founder and artistic director Dennis Foon has presented plays on subjects such as divorce (Joe Wiesenfeld's *Hilary's Birthday*), learning disabilities (John Lazarus' *Not so Dumb*), nuclear war (Colin Thomas' *One Thousand Cranes*), and sexual abuse (Thomas' *Feeling Yes, Feeling No*).

The quality of Canadian theatre for young people has been tested and enhanced by exposure to international activity. The Vancouver International Children's Festival began in 1978 and has been instrumental in bringing to Vancouver and other Canadian cities theatre companies and performers from around the world. The event has also facilitated foreign tours by Canadian companies. Mermaid Theatre, for example, appeared at the International Puppet Festival in 1984, and Green Thumb toured Hong Kong, Singapore, Australia, and New Zealand in 1985.

Developments in commercial theatre over the last decade include the success of Toronto theatre impresarios Ed and David Mirvish in turning the Royal Alexandra Theatre into something more than a touring stop for second-rate American companies. Although Canadian *plays* are still a rarity at the Alex, Canadian *productions* are frequent, whether they be transfers from the Stratford or Shaw Festivals (*The Mikado* in 1983, *Cyrano de Bergerac* in 1984) or original productions such as Tom Stoppard's *The Real Thing* in 1985, starring R.H. Thompson and directed by Guy Sprung. Productions from abroad still regularly play the Alex; many of them are humdrum, but some are theatrical coups—the visit of the Berliner Ensemble in 1986 (its first-ever appearance in North America), or the English Shakespeare Company of Michael Bogdanov and Michael Pennington in 1987, for example.

Commercial theatre activity in Toronto was further boosted by the success of the Andrew Lloyd Webber musical *Cats*, which opened in March 1985. Producers Marlene Smith and Tina VanderHeyden raised $3 million from private sources to mount an all-Canadian production in the refurbished Elgin Theatre (built in 1913); pre-opening sales were almost $4 million. A less ambitious independent production of the musical *Little Shop of Horrors* in 1985 at the Crest Theatre in Toronto lost money, however.

Another feature of commercial theatre activity has been the growth of dinner theatres. Although many professional companies offer lunchtime theatre, to which audience members are invited to bring their lunch—Montreal's Instant Theatre began the practice in 1965, followed, for example, by Vancouver's City Stage in 1972, Calgary's Lunchbox Theatre in 1975, and Edmonton's Northern Light Theatre, also in 1975—dinner theatre is significantly different. Led by Stage West, founded in Edmonton in 1975 and now with franchises in Edmonton, Calgary, and Mississauga, dinner theatre provides a full dinner and an after-dinner play for the admission price (which can be as high as $50 per person). The plays are light fare: British sex comedies and simple musicals are popular, often starring American television personalities.

In contrast to the high finance of contemporary Canadian commercial theatre are the low budget one-person shows that have become common in Canadian theatres in the 1980s. John Gray's *Billy Bishop Goes to War*, a play about Canada's First World War flying ace, has been performed by Eric Peterson (with John Gray at the piano) across Canada and in London and New York. Linda Griffiths has had considerable success with *Maggie and Pierre*, a play about the Trudeaus that she and Paul Thompson devised; Ken Mitchell's *Gone the Burning Sun* is a powerful portrayal of Norman Bethune; a selection of sixteen monologues by Antonine Maillet, *La Sagouine* has been performed with great success in both French and English by Viola Léger; Munroe Scott's *McClure* is a stage biography of United Church missionary Robert McClure; Kenneth Brown's *Life After Hockey* was the hit of the 1985 Edmonton Fringe Festival Theatre Event. These and other one-person plays depend heavily on effective acting and directing to sustain audience interest in one character, but at their best (as in *Billy Bishop* and *Gone the Burning Sun*) they can evoke a subtlety of characterization and variety of incident that belie the apparent limitations of their form.

Edmonton's Fringe Festival was founded in 1982 by Brian Paisley, and by 1986 this annual event had grown so dramatically that thirteen theatres mounted some 130 productions from noon to midnight before thousands of spectators. Together with plays from abroad, many new Canadian works are offered at the Festival. Montreal's Theatre Festival of the Americas is a still more recent addition to Canadian theatre festivals. In 1987 Canadian works such as Peter Eliot Weiss's *The Haunted House Hamlet* (produced by Vancouver's Tamahnous Theatre) and Hillar Listoja's *This is What Happens in Orangeville* (DNA Theatre, Toronto) were showcased.

Contemporary Canadian theatre has been further enriched by the consolidation and growth of multicultural companies. With a history going back to the major influx of immigrants to Canada in the early 1900s, ethnic theatre groups have established firm identities in many Canadian cities, and several new groups have emerged to extend the work of well-established companies, such as the Deutsches Theater of Montreal (founded in 1952), the Yiddish Theatre of Montreal (1956), and Winnipeg's Ukrainian Dramatic Ensemble (1956). Newer companies include Montreal's Le Maschère (1974), Vancouver's

German Theatre (1971) and Jewish Heritage Theatre (1972), Winnipeg's Mennonite Theatre (1972), Edmonton's Ukrainian Story Theatre for Children (1979), and Toronto's Black Theatre Canada (1973) and Leah Posluns Theatre (1977). These and many other companies (some 350 altogether) belong to the National Multicultural Theatre Association (founded in 1975), which sponsors a vibrant annual festival of Canadian multicultural theatre.

An important complement to a strong theatrical culture—in addition to the need for funding agencies, like the Canada Council, and training institutions, such as the National Theatre School—is a support infrastructure of awards, professional organizations, theatre publishers, and educational projects. When the Governor General's Literary Awards were instituted in 1937 no separate category recognized drama. Not until 1981 was such a category established for best published plays (English and French) of the year—won in the first year by Sharon Pollock's *Blood Relations and Other Plays* and Marie Laberge's *C'Etait avant la guerre à L'Anse à Gilles*. This was preceded by the Clifford E. Lee National Playwriting Awards (1974–81) in Edmonton, and the Chalmers Canadian Play Awards, established in 1972 by the Floyd S. Chalmers Foundation to recognize outstanding plays produced in the Metropolitan Toronto area. The Dora Mavor Moore Awards for outstanding production, directing, performance, and design in Metropolitan Toronto were established in 1979, and in Vancouver the Jessie Richardson Theatre Awards for theatre artists were first presented in 1983.

Professional organizations such as Playwrights Canada, the Association of Canadian Designers, the Canadian Theatre Critics Association, the Professional Association of Canadian Theatres, and Canadian Actors' Equity Association protect and promote the interests of theatre professionals. Playwrights Canada is also an important publisher of Canadian plays, as are Talonbooks in Vancouver, NeWest Press in Edmonton, Borealis Press in Ottawa, Coach House Press and Simon and Pierre in Toronto. Three national journals are devoted to the study and appreciation of Canadian drama and theatre: *Canadian Theatre Review* (founded in 1974), *Canadian Drama, L'Art dramatique canadien* (1975), and *Theatre History in Canada/Histoire du théâtre au Canada* (1980). Recent anthologies of Canadian plays—Richard Plant's *Penguin Book of Modern Canadian Drama* (1984), Richard

Perkyns' *Major Plays of the Canadian Theatre 1934-1984* (1984), and Jerry Wasserman's *Modern Canadian Plays* (1985)—have stimulated the study of Canadian drama in community colleges and universities. The universities have also taken strong initiatives to collect, preserve, and make available for research theatre archival material. The University of Calgary has the manuscripts of many Canadian playwrights, particularly those from western Canada; the papers of Mavor Moore, Herman Voaden, and Roy Mitchell are at York University; those of John Herbert at the University of Waterloo and of John Coulter at McMaster University. York also houses CBC television scripts, while CBC radio scripts are at Concordia University. Dalhousie University has the archives of Halifax's Neptune Theatre, and Memorial University established in 1983 the Newfoundland Performing Arts Archive Project. The University of Guelph has acquired the archives of many Ontario theatres, including those of the Shaw Festival. The Stratford Festival maintains its own archives, and the Metropolitan Toronto Library has developed the most comprehensive collection of Canadian theatre materials in the country. Canadian theatre scholarship was advanced by the formation of the Association for Canadian Theatre History/Association d'histoire du théâtre au Canada in 1976, and a team of scholars based at the University of Guelph has embarked on the formidable task of creating a data-base, Records of Canadian Theatre, recording all professional theatre activity in Canada from the eighteenth century to the present.

It would be misleading to give the impression that there have not been setbacks to Canadian theatre in the 1970s and 1980s. Funding problems remain acute for many theatre companies, and some have collapsed: Open Circle, NDWT, and Phoenix in Toronto; Festival Lennoxville; Theatre 3 in Edmonton; Theatre 2000 in Ottawa; English-language productions at the National Arts Centre. New companies, however, continue to appear, and although there has been no new theatre-building boom to compare with that of the 1960s, important theatres such as the Sudbury Theatre Centre, the Northern Arts and Culture Centre in Yellowknife, and the Calgary Centre for the Performing Arts have opened in the 1980s. Restorations of historic theatres such as Toronto's Elgin and Winter Garden, the Imperial-Capitol in Saint John, and the King's Playhouse in Georgetown, P.E.I., have been completed or are underway. But perhaps a theatre restoration completed in London, England, in 1983 is a more revealing example of the new status of Canadian theatre. When the refurbished Old Vic re-opened that year, the venerable British institution—built in 1818— was under the control of a Canadian, Toronto businessman Ed Mirvish. For Mirvish the purchase was a business gamble; for Canadian theatre it was a grand symbolic act of independence—the colonized had become the colonizers.

* * * * * *

In 1769 Mrs Frances Brooke recorded her conviction that 'The rigour of the climate [in Canada] suspends the very powers of the understanding; what then must become of those of the imagination?' It has been one of the purposes of this study to show that the factors militating against the creation of an indigenous Canadian theatre were cultural and political, not climatic, and that Canadians were long denied—or denied themselves—full imaginative expression in drama and theatre. 'In order to achieve any semblance of nationhood on a consolidated basis,' George Ryga argues, 'we have to redefine some mythological reason—which we can all agree on—for why we do the things the way we do them.' In this century Canadian dramatists have attempted to redefine the past (in order to say something about the present), reaching back to key historical figures—Riel, Sitting Bull, the Donnellys, Billy Bishop, Bethune. But they have also created a gallery of memorable characters whose collective portrait is a portrait of Canada: mad Hester in *Still Stands the House*, the doomed Rita Joe, the Mercer family. In his conclusion to the second edition of the *Literary History of Canada* (1976) Northrop Frye characterized Canadian literary history as a record of 'an emerging form of Canadian self-definition' that involved 'looking at the difference from the American parallel development'. He links Canada's Confederation centenary (1967) with the bicentenary of the American Revolution (1976), and while speculating that the American Empire was now on the decline, he writes of how Canada 'traditionally so diffident, introverted, past-and-future fixated, incoherent, inarticulate, proceeding by hunch and feeling, seems to be taking on, at least culturally, an inner composure and integration of outlook, even some buoyancy and confidence.' The point can be illustrated strikingly by two Canadian plays. Earlier we saw how Robertson Davies' protagonist in *Fortune, My Foe* was tempted to leave Canada to seek cultural and intellectual fulfilment in the United States. Thirty years later David French treated a similar theme in *Jitters*, but the resolution is handled differently and in a way that illustrates the new-found 'buoyancy and confidence' Frye has attributed to Canadians. While preparing for the opening night of their new Canadian play, the company in *Jitters* anxiously await the arrival of a famous New York producer, Bernie Feldman. Like Godot, Feldman does not arrive; the closing lines of the play comment on that non-arrival:

PHIL: George, Feldman was my only hope; he was an American. Down there they embrace success. Up here it's like stepping out of line.

GEORGE: Phil, get off the stage.
           (*Phil . . . starts to exit . . .*)

GEORGE: Hey Phil . . .
           Just remember; he's not the only producer in New York.

PHIL: I know, but he was single and the right age. I thought I had my mother all lined up.

The humour and self-deprecation in that exchange—in contrast to the pain and frustration in Davies' play—point to real growth and maturity in Canadian theatre.

BROOKE. FRANCES. *The History of Emily Montague. Canadian Anthology*, ed. C.F. Klinck and R.E. Watters. Toronto, Gage, 1966.

DAVIES. ROBERTSON. 'A Dialogue: The State of Theatre in Canada.' Reprinted in *Canadian Theatre Review*, 5 (Winter 1975), 16–36.

ELIOT, T.S. 'Poetry and Drama.' *Selected Prose*, ed. John Haywood. London, Penguin, 1955.

FRATICELLI, RINA. 'The Status of Women in the Canadian Theatre.' Report prepared for the Status of Women Canada. 1982. Unpublished. Extracts are printed in *Fuse*, 6 (September 1982).

FRYE. NORTHROP. 'Conclusion'. *Literary History of Canada*. 2nd ed. General Editor, C.F. Klinck. Toronto, University of Toronto Press, 1976.

KAPLAN, JON. '*Tamara* Takes Off.' *Canadian Theatre Review*, 44 (Fall 1985), 135–8.

KEITH, W.J. *Canadian Literature in English*. London and New York, Longman, 1985.

INNES, CHRISTOPHER. 'The Many Faces of Rita Joe: The Anatomy of a Playwright's Development.' *Canadian Drama, L'Art dramatique canadien*, 10 (1984), 145–66.

NUNN, ROBERT. 'Sharon Pollock's Plays: A Review Article.' *Theatre History in Canada/ Histoire du théâtre au Canada*, 5 (1984), 72–83.

SALUTIN, RICK. An interview with Cynthia Zimmerman in *The Work: Conversations with English–Canadian Playwrights*, ed. Robert Wallace and Cynthia Zimmerman. Toronto, Coach House Press, 1982.

SHAKESPEARE, WILLIAM. *Sonnets*. Ed. Edward Bliss Reed. New Haven, Yale University Press, 1961. The text of sonnet 29 printed in *Fortune and Men's Eyes* contains two changes from Shakespeare's: Shakespeare's 'state' (line 10) becomes 'soul' and his 'change' (line 14) becomes 'share'.

SMITH, PATRICIA KEENEY. 'Living with Risk: Toronto's New Alternate Theatre.' *Canadian Theatre Review*, 38 (Fall 1983), 33–43.

STUART, ROSS. 'The Crest Controversy.' *Canadian Theatre Review*, 7 (Summer 1975), 8–11. For quotations on the Crest's mandate and for the Canada Council press release see 'A Chronological Commentary' in the same issue of *CTR*.

WASSERMAN, JERRY, ed. *Modern Canadian Plays*. Vancouver, Talonbooks, 1985.

WATSON, DAVID and CHRISTOPHER INNES. 'Political Mythologies: An Interview with George Ryga.' *Canadian Drama, L'Art dramatique canadien*, 8 (1982), 160–72.

SELECTED BIBLIOGRAPHY

REFERENCE WORKS

BALL, JOHN and RICHARD PLANT. *A Bibliography of Canadian Theatre History 1583–1975.* Anton Wagner, gen. ed. Toronto, Playwrights Co-op, 1976.

BALL, JOHN and RICHARD PLANT, eds. *The Bibliography of Canadian Theatre History Supplement 1975–1976.* Toronto, Playwrights Co-op, 1979.

BULLER, EDWARD. *Indigenous Performing and Ceremonial Arts in Canada: A Bibliography. An Annotated Bibliography of Canadian Indian Rituals and Ceremonies (up to 1976).* Toronto, Association for Native Development in the Performing and Visual Arts, 1981.

Canadian Encyclopedia, The, 3 vols. Edmonton, Hurtig, 1985.

FINK, HOWARD, with BRIAN MORRISON. *Canadian National Theatre on the Air 1925–1961. CBC-CRBC-CNR Radio Drama in English: A Descriptive Bibliography and Union List.* Toronto, University of Toronto Press, 1983.

McCALLUM, HEATHER. *Research Collections in Canadian Libraries.* Special Studies: 1. Theatre Resources in Canadian Collections. Ottawa, National Library of Canada, 1973.

O'NEILL, PATRICK. 'A Checklist of Canadian Dramatic Materials to 1967.' Parts I and II in *Canadian Drama, L'Art dramatique canadien,* 8 (1982), 173–303, and 9 (1983), 369–506.

Playwrights Union of Canada Catalogue of Canadian Plays. Toronto, Playwrights Union of Canada, 1985.

RUBIN, DON and ALISON CRANMER-BYNG, eds. *Canada's Playwrights: A Biographical Guide.* Toronto, CTR Publications, 1980.

RUBIN, DON, ed. *Canada On Stage: Canadian Theatre Review Yearbook.* 8 vols. Downsview, Ont., CTR Publications, 1974–1982.

TOYE, WILLIAM, gen. ed. *The Oxford Companion to Canadian Literature.* Toronto, Oxford University Press, 1983.

WAGNER, ANTON, ed. *The Brock Bibliography of Published Canadian Plays in English, 1766–1978.* Toronto, Playwrights Press, 1980.

COLLECTIONS OF PLAYS

BEISSEL, HENRY, ed. *Cues and Entrances: Ten Canadian One-Act Plays.* Toronto, Gage, 1977.

BENSON, EUGENE, ed. *Encounter: Canadian Drama in Four Media.* Toronto, Methuen, 1973.

BESSAI, DIANE and DON KERR, eds. *Showing West. Three Prairie Docu-Dramas*. Edmonton, NeWest, 1982.

BESSAI, DIANE, ed. *Prairie Performance: A Collection of Short Plays*. Edmonton, NeWest, 1980.

Canadian Plays for Young Audiences. Toronto, Playwrights Union of Canada, 1984.

CARSON, NEIL, ed. *New Canadian Drama*. Ottawa, Borealis Press, 1980.

FINK, HOWARD and JOHN JACKSON, eds. *All the Bright Company: Radio Drama Produced by Andrew Allan*. Toronto and Kingston, CBC Enterprises and Quarry Press, 1987.

KALMAN, ROLF, ed. *A Collection of Canadian Plays*. 5 vols. Toronto, Simon & Pierre, 1972-8.

LESCARBOT, MARC. *Le Théâtre de Neptune en La Nouvelle-France*. *Canadian Drama, L'Art dramatique canadien*, 7 (1981), 44-50.

———. *The Theatre of Neptune in New France*. Translated by Eugene Benson and Renate Benson. *Canada's Lost Plays*. Vol. 4, ed. Anton Wagner. Toronto. CTR Publications, 1982.

MASSEY, VINCENT, ed. *Canadian Plays from Hart House Theatre*. 2 vols. Toronto, Macmillan, 1926-7.

O'NEILL, PATRICK, ed. *New Canadian Drama -2*. Ottawa, Borealis Press, 1981.

PERKYNS, RICHARD, ed. *Major Plays of the Canadian Theatre 1934-1984*. Toronto, Irwin, 1984.

PLANT, RICHARD, ed. *The Penguin Book of Modern Canadian Drama*. Markham, Ont., Penguin Books Canada, 1984.

SALTER, DENIS, ed. *New Canadian Drama -3*. Ottawa, Borealis Press, 1984.

SMITH, MARY ELIZABETH, ed. 'Three Political Dramas from New Brunswick.' *Canadian Drama, L'Art dramatique canadien*, 12 (1986), 144-228.

VOADEN, HERMAN, ed. *Six Canadian Plays*. Toronto, Copp Clark, 1930.

WAGNER, ANTON and RICHARD PLANT, eds. *Canada's Lost Plays, Volume One: The Nineteenth Century*. Toronto, CTR Publications, 1978.

WAGNER, ANTON, ed. *Canada's Lost Plays, Volume Two: Women Pioneers*. Toronto, CTR Publications, 1979.

———, ed. *Canada's Lost Plays, Volume Three: The Developing Mosaic: English-Canadian Drama to Mid-Century*. Toronto, CTR Publications, 1980.

———, ed. *Canada's Lost Plays, Volume Four: Colonial Quebec: French-Canadian Drama, 1606 to 1966*. Toronto, CTR Publications, 1982.

WASSERMAN, JERRY, ed. *Modern Canadian Plays*. Vancouver, Talonbooks, 1985.

WILSON, MARIAN M., ed. *Popular Performance Plays of Canada*. Toronto, Simon & Pierre, 1976.

WRIGHT, RICHARD and ROBIN ENDRES, eds. *Eight Men Speak and Other Plays from the Canadian Workers' Theatre*. Toronto, New Hogtown Press, 1976.

HISTORY AND CRITICISM

ALLAN, ANDREW. *A Self-Portrait*. Toronto, Macmillan, 1974.

ANTHONY, GERALDINE. *Gwen Pharis Ringwood*. Boston, Twayne, 1981.

——. *John Coulter*. Boston, G.K. Hall, 1976.

——, ed. *Stage Voices. Twelve Canadian Playwrights Talk About Their Lives and Work*. Toronto, Doubleday Canada, 1978.

BESSAI, DIANE. 'The Regionalism of Canadian Drama.' *Canadian Literature*, 85 (1980), 7–20.

——. 'Documentary Theatre in Canada: An Investigation into Questions and Backgrounds.' *Canadian Drama, L'Art dramatique canadien*, 6 (1980), 9–21.

BROWN, J. FREDERICK. 'The Charlottetown Festival in Review.' *Canadian Drama, L'Art dramatique canadien*, 9 (1983), 227–368.

——. 'The Charlottetown Festival in Review: An Update.' *Canadian Drama, L'Art dramatique canadien*, 12 (1986), 75–142.

BRYDEN, RONALD, with BOYD NEIL, eds. *Whittaker's Theatre: A Critic Looks at Stages in Canada and Thereabouts, 1944–1975*. Greenbank, Ont., The Whittaker Project, 1985.

CONOLLY, L.W., ed. *Theatrical Touring and Founding in North America*. Westport, Connecticut, Greenwood Press, 1982.

——, ed. 'Modern Canadian Drama: Some Critical Perspectives.' *Canadian Drama, L'Art dramatique canadien*, 11 (1985), 1–229.

DOHERTY, BRIAN. *Not Bloody Likely. The Shaw Festival 1962–1973*. Toronto, Dent, 1974.

DOOLITTLE, JOYCE and ZINA BARNIEH, with HELENE BEAUCHAMP. *A Mirror of Our Dreams: Children and the Theatre in Canada*. Vancouver, Talonbooks, 1979.

DOUCETTE, LEONARD E. *Theatre in French Canada: Laying the Foundations 1606–1867*. Toronto, University of Toronto Press, 1984.

EDMONSTONE, WAYNE. *Nathan Cohen. The Making of a Critic*. Toronto, Lester and Orpen, 1977.

EDWARDS, MURRAY D. *A Stage in Our Past. English-language Theatre in Eastern Canada from the 1790s to 1914*. Toronto, University of Toronto Press, 1968.

EVANS, CHAD. *Frontier Theatre: A History of Nineteenth-Century Theatrical Entertainment in the Canadian Far West and Alaska*. Victoria, Sono Nis, 1983.

GRAHAM, FRANKLIN. *Histrionic Montreal. Annals of the Montreal Stage with Biographical and Critical Notices of the Plays and Players of a Century.* 2nd ed. Montreal, Lovell, 1902.

INNES, CHRISTOPHER. *Politics and the Playwright: George Ryga.* Toronto, Simon & Pierre, 1985.

KNELMAN, MARTIN. *A Stratford Tempest.* Toronto, McClelland and Stewart, 1982.

LEE, BETTY. *Love and Whisky: The Story of the Dominion Drama Festival.* Toronto, McClelland and Stewart, 1973 and Toronto, Simon and Pierre, 1982.

LINDSAY, JOHN C. *'Turn Out the Stars Before Leaving': The Story of Canada's Theatres.* Erin, Ont., Boston Mills Press, 1983.

NARDOCCHIO, ELAINE. *Theatre and Politics in Modern Quebec.* Edmonton, University of Alberta Press, 1986.

NEW, WILLIAM H., ed. *Dramatists in Canada: Selected Essays.* Vancouver, University of British Columbia Press, 1972.

ORRELL, JOHN. *Fallen Empires: Lost Theatres of Edmonton 1881-1914.* Edmonton, NeWest, 1981.

PETTIGREW, JOHN and JAMIE PORTMAN. *Stratford: the First Thirty Years.* 2 vols. Toronto, Macmillan, 1985.

RIPLEY, JOHN. 'Drama and Theatre, 1960-73.' *Literary History of Canada,* 2nd ed. Ed. Carl F. Klinck. Toronto, University of Toronto Press, 1976, III, 212-32.

RITTENHOUSE, JONATHAN. 'Festival Lennoxville: An All-Canadian Story.' *Canadian Drama, L'Art dramatique canadien,* 10 (1984), 84-114.

Royal Commission Studies: A Selection of Essays Prepared for the Royal Commission on National Development in the Arts, Letters and Sciences. Ottawa, Edmond Cloutier, 1951.

RYAN, TOBY GORDON. *Stage Left: Canadian Theatre in the Thirties: A Memoir.* Toronto, CTR Publications, 1981, and Toronto, Simon & Pierre, 1985.

SADDLEMYER, ANN. 'Circus Feminus: 100 Plays by English-Canadian Women.' *Room of One's Own,* 8 (1983), 78-91.

SMITH, MARY ELIZABETH. *Too Soon the Curtain Fell: A History of Theatre in Saint John 1789-1900.* Fredericton, Brunswick Press, 1981.

STONE-BLACKBURN, SUSAN. *Robertson Davies, Playwright. A Search for the Self on the Canadian Stage.* Vancouver, University of British Columbia Press, 1985.

STUART, E. ROSS. *The History of Prairie Theatre: The Development of Theatre in Alberta, Manitoba and Saskatchewan 1833-1982.* Toronto, Simon & Pierre, 1984.

TAIT, MICHAEL. 'Drama and Theatre, 1920-1960.' *Literary History of Canada,* 2nd ed. Ed. Carl F. Klinck. Toronto, University of Toronto Press, 1976, II, 143-67.

USMIANI, RENATE. *Second Stage: The Alternative Theatre Movement in Canada*. Vancouver, University of British Columbia Press, 1983.

WAGNER, ANTON, ed. *Contemporary Canadian Theatre: New World Visions*. Toronto, Simon & Pierre, 1985.

WALLACE, ROBERT and CYNTHIA ZIMMERMAN. *The Work: Conversations with English-Canadian Playwrights*. Toronto, Coach House Press, 1982.

INDEX

Abbey Theatre, 45, 53
Abroad and at Home, 3
Academy of Music, 10, 16
Acadius; or, Love in a Calm, 4
Actors' Colony, 68, 69
Actor's Playhouse, 73
Adams, Maude, 29
Adventure Theatre, 74
Agitprop theatre, 58, 87
Aikins, Carroll, 48, 49
A.K.A. Performance Interfaces, 105
Albee, Edward, 80, 84, 91
Alberta Theatre Projects, 85, 99, 102
Aldous, J.E.P., 18
Alexander Mackenzie, 48
Alianak, Hrant, 89
Allan, Andrew, 46, 60-1, 69
Allan, Martha, 53
Allen, Edward, 34
Allen Players, 44
Allen, Ted, 69
Alligator Pie, 108
All's Well That Ends Well, 70
All the World's a Stage, 4
Alternate theatre, 85-9, 91, 103, 104, 105
American Company of Comedians, 7, 34
American Modern, 107
Anglin, Margaret, 29, 33, 39
Anne of Green Gables, 108
Anthony, Geraldine, 56
Antigone, 39
Archives (theatre), 112
Arliss, George, 29
Arnold, Charles, 27
Artaud, Antonin, 86
Arthur, Julia, 33, 38, 39
Artichoke, 107
Art of War, The, 92, 93
Arts and Culture Centre, 73, 96
Arts and Letters Club, 45, 53

Arts and Letters Players, 45, 46, 51
As For Me and My House, 47
Association for Canadian Theatre History, 112
Association of Canadian Designers, 111
As You Like It, 29
At My Heart's Core, 55
Audiences, 21-3, 25, 35, 57, 74
Automatic Pilot, 107
Avon Theatre, 71, 73, 77, 78

Bach, J.S., 62
Bagdad Saloon, 91
Balconville, 72, 98-9
Balm, 48
Bandmann, Daniel, 38
Banff Centre School of Fine Arts, 63
Banff School of Fine Arts, 63, 64, 82
Barrett, Lawrence, 34
Barrett, Wilson, 39
Barrie, J.M., 29
Bathurst St Theatre, 79
Battering Ram, 88, 89, 90
Bayly, T.H., 3
Beaverbrook Theatre, 83
Beck, Julian, 85
Beckett, Samuel, 70, 84
Behan, Brendan, 80
Beissel, Henry, 76, 77
Ben Hur, 33
Benson, Frank, 29
Beresford-Howe, Constance, 77
Berliner Ensemble, 109
Bernard, John, 9, 11, 34
Bernhardt, Sarah, 22, 29, 99
Bessai, Diane, 96, 103
Bessborough, Earl of, 52
Bethune, Norman, 82, 102, 103, 110, 113
Better Living, 93, 104
Beyond Mozambique, 91
Bickerstaffe, Isaac, 10

Big Boom, The, 31
Billboard, 37
Billy Bishop and the Red Baron, 108
Billy Bishop Goes to War, 72, 110
Birmingham Repertory Theatre, 32, 48
Black, Malcolm, 69, 80
Black, Thomas, 19
Black Feather, The, 14
Black Powder, 84
Black Rock Theatre, 98
Black Theatre Canada, 111
Blanchard, Kitty, 38
Blood Relations, 100, 101–2
Blood Relations and Other Plays, 102, 111
Bloomfield, George, 81
Bluma Appel Theatre, 83
Blyth Festival, 84
Bogdanov, Michael, 109
Bolt, Carol, 72, 88, 104, 107, 108
Bonheur d'occasion, 97
Book of Eve, The, 77
Booth, Edwin, 34
Booth, Michael, 26
Borealis Press, 111
Borsook, Henry, 48
Bowles, N.W., 58
Boyle, Harry, 69
Brecht, Bertolt, 58
Breed of the Treshams, The, 30
British-Canadian Theatrical Organization, 30, 32
British Colonist, 25
Brock Bibliography, The, 20
Brooke, Frances, 113
Brookes, Chris, 87
Brothers in Arms, 46, 48
Broughall, George, 30, 31
Brown, Frederick, 10
Brown, Kenneth, 110
Brown, Mary, 33
Buck, Tim, 58
Buddies in Bad Times, 105
Buffalo Jump, 107
Bulwer-Lytton, Edward, 34

Burlap Bags, 61
Burroughs, Jackie, 69
Bury the Dead, 57
Bush, Thomas, 14

Caldwell, Erskine, 68
Calgary Centre for the Performing Arts, 112
Callaghan, Morley, 69
Camille, 29
Campbell, Archibald, 5
Campbell, Douglas, 69, 73
Campbell, Lockie, 51
Campbell, Mrs Patrick, 35
Campbell, Paddy, 108
Campbell, Wilfred, 11, 13
Canada Council, 68, 70, 71, 72, 83, 84, 111
Canada's Lost Plays, 16
Canada's Welcome, 15, 16
Canadian Actors' Equity Association, 111
Canadian Arts Council, 49
Canadian Bookman, 45, 46
Canadian Brothers, The, 78
Canadian Conference of the Arts, 49
Canadian Courant, 22
Canadian Drama, L'Art dramatique canadien, 111
Canadian Forum, 51, 55
Canadian Gothic, 107
Canadian Illustrated News, 20
Canadian Literature, 96
Canadian Magazine, 13, 26, 37, 43
Canadian Plays from Hart House, 48
Canadian Radio Broadcasting Commission, 59
Canadian Theatre Critics Association, 111
Canadian Theatre Review, 103, 105, 111
Canadian West Monthly, 37
Cannibal performance (see Hamatsa), 1
Canvas Barricade, The, 77
Capitol Theatre, 44

Caplan, Henry, 69
Caplan, Rupert, 51, 60
Captives of the Faceless Drummer, 81
Carle, Richard, 25
'Caroli Candidus', 16
Carolina Playmakers, 64
Cats, 109
Cavafy, 105
'CBC Wednesday Night', 61
Cecil-Smith, Edward, 58
Celine, Louis-Ferdinand, 75
Censorship, 3, 21, 59, 68
Centaur Theatre, 84, 97, 98
CentreStage, 83, 91, 93, 100, 104
C'Était avant la guerre à L'Anse à Gilles, 111
Chalmers Award, 74, 90, 99, 111
Chalmers Foundation, Floyd S., 111
Champlain, Samuel, 2
Charlesworth, Hector, 22, 39
Charlesworth, Marigold, 69
Charlottetown Festival, 73, 108
Chautauqua, 26, 103
Chautauqua Girl, 103
Chekhov, Anton, 70, 77, 91, 95, 100, 102, 104
Cheney, B.P., 38
Chicago '70, 85
Chichester Festival, 71
Chilcott, Barbara, 70
Children's theatre, 68, 76, 108–9
Chislett, Anne, 88, 107
Chris Axelson, Blacksmith, 64
Christie, Robert, 62
Ciceri, Leo, 69, 72
Cigarette Maker's Romance, The, 30
Citadel Theatre, 7, 72, 73, 83, 84, 101
City Stage, 109
Clifford E. Lee National Playwriting Awards, 111
Coach House Press, 111
Cockings, George, 4
Codco, 85
Coe, Peter, 7, 84
Coghill, Joy, 80

Colicos, John, 53, 62
Collectives, 86–8, 105, 107
Colonial Theatre, 25
Colours in the Dark, 73, 76, 77, 83
Colour the Flesh the Colour of Dust, 96
Colville, Alex, 107
Commercial theatre, 109
Community Players of Winnipeg, 49
Cone, Tom, 77
Conquest of Canada, The, 4
Cook, Michael, 60, 96–7, 98
Cooke, Britton, 48
Cormon, Eugène, 38
Corneille, Pierre, 3
Coulter, John, 52, 53–4, 57, 64, 69, 112
Count Filippo, 12
Courting of Marie Jenvrin, The, 64
Covent Garden Theatre, 4
Coward, Noel, 84
Cowells, The, 9
Crabdance, 107
Crackwalker, The, 107
Creative Theatre, 45
Creeps, 88, 89, 90, 91
Crest Theatre, 55, 69–70, 109
Crime of Louis Riel, The, 54
Criminals in Love, 93
Cruel Tears, 103
Culture, 63
Curtain Call, 51
Curzon, Sarah Anne, 13
Cushing, Eliza Lanesford, 14
Cushman, Charlotte, 12
Cyclone Jack, 108
Cyrano de Bergerac, 109

Dagger and the Cross, The, 15
Daily Colonist, 26
Danites, The, 38
D'Annunzio, Gabriele, 105
Dark Harvest, 64
Daulac, 13
Davies, Robertson, 52, 54–7, 64, 69, 70, 71, 73, 114
Davin, N.F., 18, 102

Davin: the Politician, 18, 102
Daviot, Gordon, 69
Davis, Donald, 46, 69, 70
Davis, Murray, 46, 69, 70
Day of Victory, 61
Death, 88
Death of a Salesman, 94
Deep Thought, 88
De la Roche, Mazo, 69
Del Grande, Louis, 89
Delicatessen, 104
Denison, Merrill, 45–8, 49, 50, 60, 64, 96
D'Ennery, Adolphe, 38
Deptford trilogy, 56
De Roberval, 14
Deutsches Theater (Montreal), 110
Deux orphelines, Les, 38
Deverell, Rex, 84, 108
Dexter, John, 7, 84
Dickens, Charles, 30
Dinner theatre, 109
Dionysus in '69, 85
Diplomacy, 39
Dixon, F.A., 15
DNA Theatre, 110
Doc, 102
Dolorsolatio, 16, 17, 18
Dominion Drama Festival, 51–3, 54, 55, 57
Dominion Stock Company, 44
Donnellys, The, 78–9, 89, 92
Dora Awards, 105, 111
Douglas, 7
Drainie, John, 62, 69
Dramatist, The, 10
Dreaming and Duelling, 108
Dressler, Marie, 39
Drums Are Out, The, 53
Drury Lane (London), 4
Drury Lane Theatre (Saint John), 3, 5
Dubé, Marcel, 69
Dyott, William, 3

Earl Grey Musical and Dramatic Competition, 51

Earth Song, 50
Easter Egg, The, 76
East Lynne, 37
'E.B.', 24
Eckhardt Players, 44
Ecstasy of Rita Joe, The, 73, 80–1
Edwards, Mae, 44
Edwards, Murray, 11
1837: The Farmers' Revolt, 87
Eight Men Speak, 58–9
Electra, 39
Elgin and Winter Garden Theatres, 112
Elgin Theatre, 109
Eliot, George, 78
Eliot, T.S., 82
Eliot, William, 4
Empire Theatre, 39
Empress Company, 44
Empress of Ireland, 30
Enamorado, The, 14
English Shakespeare Company, 109
Erickson, Nola, 103
Eros at Breakfast, 54
Esker Mike and his Wife, Agiluk, 88
Esther, a Sacred Drama, 14
Euripides, 39
Eve, 77
Ever Loving, 107
Everyman, 80
Everyman Theatre Company, 68, 69
Explorations program, 71
Expressionism, 49–51
Extra Space, 105

Factory Theatre, 12, 93
Factory Theatre Lab, 85, 88, 89, 91, 93
Fairbanks Wharf Theatre, 7
Fair Grit, The, 16, 18
Falconer, Edmund, 22
Family Portrait, The, 53
Far As the Eye Can See, 104
Farm Show, The, 87
Farrar, Geraldine, 29
Farther West, 100
Faust, 29
Federal Street Theatre, 34

Feeling Yes, Feeling No, 108
Female Consistory of Brockville, The, 16
Feminist theatre, 107
Fennario, David, 72, 84, 88, 96, 97
Festival Lennoxville, 84, 96, 112
Festival of Underground Theatre, 85
Festival Theatre (Stratford), 71, 77
Fiddle, Faddle and Foozle, 21
Fifine, the Fisher-Maid, 15
Filthy Rich, 92
Findley, Timothy, 60
Fineberg, Larry, 77, 88
Fink, Howard, 60
Fisher, Charles, 22
Fiske, Minnie, 29, 34
Five-Minute Feminist Cabaret, 107
Flytrap, 91
Foon, Dennis, 108
Forbes-Robertson, J., 29, 30
Forever Yours, Marie-Lou, 89
Fortune and Men's Eyes, 73–5, 76, 77, 83, 90
Fortune, My Foe, 54, 55, 114
Fortune of War, The, 21
Fox, David, 103
Frank's Hotel, 21
Fraticelli, Rina, 107
Fredericton Loyalist, 5
Freedom of Jean Guichet, The, 48
Freeman, David, 88–91
French, David, 60, 89, 92, 93–5, 114
Fringe Festival (Edmonton), 110
From Their Own Place, 46
Frontenac, Governor, 3
'Front Row Centre', 72
Frye, Northrop, 12, 113
Fuller, W.H., 19, 20
Furies, The, 65
Futz, 85, 87

Gabe, 88
Gabriel Dumont: The Plainsman, 102
Galvin Players, 44
Galvin Producing Company, 44
Gardner, David, 69
Garrard, Jim, 86

Garrick, David, 7
Garrison theatre, 3–4, 8, 26, 30, 37
Gaspé Manifesto, 84
Gass, Ken, 88, 89, 103
Gayden Chronicles, The, 97
General Confession, 55, 56
Generations, 102
Genet, Jean, 75
George, Chief Dan, 81
German Theatre (Vancouver), 111
Gerussi, Bruno, 74
Ghosts, 24, 31
Gilbert, Humphrey, 2
Gilbert, Sky, 105
Gilbert, W.S., 19, 30
Gill, Robert, 46, 69
Gillmore, Jack, 60
Glass, Joanna, 107
Glassco, Bill, 89, 93, 94, 95, 104
Glass Menagerie, The, 94
Glazed Tempera, 107
Globe, 12, 49, 50
Globe Theatre, 72, 84, 108
God of Gods, The, 48
Goldberg, Mildred, 58
Goldoni, Carlo, 77
Goldsmith, Oliver, 56
Gone the Burning Sun, 102, 110
Gossip, 92
Government House, 15
Governor General's Literary Awards, 76, 102, 111
Gowan, Elsie Park, 60
Graham, Franklin, 22, 27
Grand Opera House (Hamilton), 16
Grand Opera House (London), 11
Grand Opera House (Ottawa), 15
Grand Opera House (Toronto), 11, 14, 36
Grant, Cynthia, 107
Grass and Wild Strawberries, 81
Gray, John, 69, 72, 110
Great Canadian Theatre Company, 105
Great Cultural Revolution, The, 103
Green, Paul, 64
Greene, Lorne, 62, 69

Green Thumb Theatre, 108, 109
Gregory, Lady Augusta, 45
Grein, J.T., 45
Griffiths, Linda, 72, 110
Grip, 20
Grip-Sack, 13
Gros Mourn, 87
Group of Seven, 40
Grove, Frederick, 64
Grove Press, 74
Guelph Spring Festival, 99, 103
Guevara, Che, 82
Gulliver's Travels, 33
Guthrie, Tyrone, 48, 53, 55, 60, 70
Guthrie Theatre, 71
Gyroscope, 78

Hackney, Mabel, 30
Hair, 85
Halifax Theatre Arts Guild, 49
Halifax Theatrical Society, 6
Hall, Amelia, 53, 69, 70
Ham, George H., 10
Hamatsa drama, 1, 2
Handcuffs, 79
Handscomb, C.W., 24, 31
Hannan, Charles, 30
Hardin, Herschel, 88
Harris, Lawren, 45
Harron, Don, 53, 62
Hart, Lorenz, 104
Hart House Theatre, 45–6, 47, 48, 49,
    51, 53, 58
Hart's Opera House, 27
Harvey, née Walker, Ruth, 27
Hatton, Joseph, 15
Haunted House Hamlet, The, 110
Hawthorne, Nathaniel, 12
Hayes, Edward, 2
Haynes, Elizabeth Sterling, 63
Hay's Theatre, 10
*Head, Guts and Sound Bone Dance,
    The*, 96
Hearst Greek Theatre, 39
Heartbreak House, 48
Heavysege, Charles, 11, 12

Hecate's Players, 107
Hedda Gabler, 70
Hendry, Tom, 53, 72, 77
Henry, Martha, 69, 100, 104
Henry V, 12
Henry Hudson, 48
Henry Hudson and Other Plays, 47
Herbert, John, 73–5, 77, 83, 112
Her Majesty's Theatre, 10
Herring, Frances, 25
Hey Rube!, 86
Hilary's Birthday, 108
Hildebrand, 13
Hill, Thomas, 5
Hill-Land, 50
Hippolytus, 39
Hirsch, John, 69, 72, 76
His Majesty's Theatre, 39
H.M.S. Parliament, 16, 19, 20, 31
H.M.S. Pinafore, 19
H.M.S. Trincomalee, 26
Hoffman, James, 2
Holden, John, 68, 69
Holiday Theatre, 107
Hollingsworth, Margaret, 107
Hollingsworth, Michael, 89, 105
Holman, Joseph, 3
Holy Manhattan, 53
Home, John, 7
Home Theatre, 48
Hope Deferred, 55
Hopley's Theatre, 5
Hosanna, 89
Hostage, The, 80
House, Eric, 69
House in the Quiet Glen, The, 53
Hubert, Cam, 107
Humphrey and the Dumptrucks, 103
Hunter Duvar, John, 14
Hunting Stuart, 55, 56
Hutt, William, 46, 53
Hyland, Frances, 53, 62, 69, 72, 81

Ibsen, Henrik, 13, 23, 24, 31, 70
I Love You, Baby Blue, 87
Imperial-Capitol Theatre, 112

Independent Theatre Club, 45
Indian, 72, 80
'Indian' trilogy, 65
Innes, Christopher, 81
Inook and the Sun, 76
Instant Theatre, 109
International Puppet Festival, 109
Iphigenia in Aulis, 39
Irving, Henry, 13, 30, 35, 38
Irving, Laurence, 30, 38

Jack, Donald, 77
Jack and the Joker, The, 64, 65
Jackman, Isaac, 3
Jackson, Barry, 32
Jackson, Hart, 38
Jacob's Wake, 96, 97
Jacob Two-Two Meets the Hooded Fang, 108
Jarvis, Maria L., 9
Jenny's Story, 107
Jerome, Jerome K., 29
Jessie Richardson Theatre Awards, 111
Jewish Heritage Theatre, 111
Jig for the Gypsy, A, 55, 70
Jitters, 95, 114
Joe Beef, 98
Joe Derry, 58
John Holden Players, 68
Jones, Emrys Maldwyn, 63
Jones, H.A., 22
Joudry, Patricia, 60
Journals (theatre), 111
Juch, Emma, 27
Judah, 22
Jukes, Mary, 69
Julius Cahn's Official Theatrical Guide, 28
Jupiter Theatre, 69
Juvenile Bostonians, 29

Kaiser, Georg, 49
Kaleidoscope Theatre, 108
Kam Theatre Lab, 82
Kareda, Urjo, 77, 78, 79, 89, 90, 104
Karloff, Boris, 44

Kean, Charles, 35
Kean, Edmund, 34, 36
Kean, Ellen, 35
Keith, W.J., 65, 76
Kellerd, John E., 29
Kemble, Fanny, 35
Kennedy's Children, 104
Killdeer, The, 76
Killdeer and Other Plays, The, 76
King, Charmion, 46, 69, 70
King's Playhouse, 112
King Whistle!, 78
Kirkland, Jack, 68
Klinck, Carl F., 13
Klondike Nugget, 26
Koch, Frederick, 64
Komagata Maru Incident, The, 101
Krapp's Last Tape, 70
Krizanc, John, 105–6
Kwakiutl Mystery Play, 2

Laberge, Marie, 111
Lady of Lyons, 34
Lambert, Betty, 107
Lambert, John, 8, 9
Lament for Harmonica, 65
Land of Promise, The, 30
Langbridge, Canon, 30
Laura Secord, 13, 48
Laurence, Margaret, 64
Lazarus, Joan, 108
Lazarus, John, 108
Leah Posluns Theatre, 111
Leaving Home, 89, 93–4
Lee, Betty, 52, 53
Lee, Dennis, 108
Lee, George Simcoe, 21
Léger, Viola, 110
Lerner, Frank, 84
Lescarbot, Marc, 2, 3, 15
Letter to My Son, A, 82
Life After Hockey, 110
Lightstone, Marilyn, 70
Lillo, Larry, 104
Lincoln, Abraham, 34
Lismer, Arthur, 45

Listen to the Wind, 76
Listoja, Hillar, 110
Literary Garland, The, 14, 20
Literary History of Canada, 113
Little Shop of Horrors, 109
Little Theatre movement, 43–51, 54, 57
Littlewood, Joan, 86
Livesay, Dorothy, 58
Living Theatre, 85
Ljungh, Esse, 60
Local Initiatives Program, 85
Lohengrin, 27
Longboat, Tom, 108
Longfellow, H.W., 12
Looking Forward, 58
Lorne, Marquis of, 15
Louise, Princess, 15
Love, Frank, 58
Love and Whisky, 52
Lunchbox Theatre, 109
Lunchtime theatre, 109
Lund, Allan, 69
Luscombe, George, 59, 69, 86
Lyceum Company, 35, 38
Lyceum Theatre (London), 38
Lyceum Theatre (Montreal), 10

McClure, 110
McClure, Robert, 110
McCowan, George, 69
Macdonald, John A., 19, 20, 100
McDougall, Gordon, 84
McDowell, E.A., 20, 31
McIlraith, Jean Newton, 18, 19
Mack, Willard, 29
MacKay, Isabel, 48
MacKay, L.A., 48
McKenna, Siobhan, 99
Mackenzie, Alexander, 19
Maclean's, 89
McLeay, Franklin, 39
Madame Butterfly, 29
Mae Edwards Players, 44
Maeterlinck, Maurice, 45
Maggie and Pierre, 72, 110
Maguire, Trevor, 58

Maiden Mona the Mermaid, 15
Mail, 10
Maillet, Antonine, 110
Mair, Charles, 11, 12, 13
Major, Leon, 69
Major Plays of the Canadian Theatre, 1934–1984, 112
Mallett, Jane, 46, 62, 69
Man in the Blue Moon, The, 69
Manitoba Free Press, 24, 25
Manitoba Sun, 31
Manitoba Theatre Centre, 72, 83, 84
Mantell, Robert B., 15, 29, 34
Manticore, The, 56
Man Who Went, The, 14
Marks, Robert, 37
Marks Brothers, 37, 39
Marsh Hay, 47
Martin-Harvey, John, 30, 35, 36, 43
Maschère, La, 111
Mason, John, 29
Mason, Lawrence, 49
Masses, 58
Massey, Vincent, 48, 71
Massey Commission, 71
Maugham, Somerset, 30
Maya, 65
Mayer, David, 2
Mazeppa, 33
Measure by Measure, 5
Medea, 39
Medicare!, 84
Medicine Line, The, 102
Memoir, 99, 100
Menken, Adah Isaacs, 33
Merchant of Venice, The, 3, 75
Mermaid Theatre, 108
Metropoliton Toronto Library, 112
Middleton, J.E., 39
Mikado, The, 109
Miller, Henry, 39
Miller, Joaquin, 38
Miller's AssemblyRoom, 9
Milton, John, 77
Mirvish, David, 109
Mirvish, Ed, 109, 113

Mis' Nelly of N'Orleans, 29
Miss in Her Teens, 7
Mitchell, Ken, 18, 96, 102–3, 110
Mitchell, Langdon, 29
Mitchell, Roy, 45, 46, 112
Mitchell, W.O., 60
Modern Canadian Plays, 112
Moiseiwitsch, Tanya, 71
Molière, Jean Baptiste, 3, 55
Molson, John, 10
Monette, Richard, 69, 74
Montcalm, 48
Montcalm, Louis Joseph, 48
Monte Carlo Theatre, 26
Montreal Repertory Theatre, 49
Moodie, Susanna, 55
Moore, Dora Mavor, 46, 68, 69
Moore, Mavor, 53, 60, 69, 72, 112
Morality and theatre, 6, 23–5
Mordred, 13
Morning, 13
Morrison, Charlotte, 36, 37
Morse, Barry, 69
Mortifee, Ann, 81
Morton, J.M., 3
Moss, Peter, 108
Mother Country, 107
Moving, 98
Mrs Warren's Profession, 24
Mulgrave Road Co-op Theatre, 105
Multicultural theatre, 110
Mummers Troupe, 59, 85, 87
Murder Pattern, 50, 51
Murrell, John, 77, 96, 99–100, 103

National Arts Centre, 72, 76, 100, 112
National Multicultural Theatre
    Association, 111
National Policy, 19
National Theatre School, 72, 111
NDWT Company, 79, 112
Necessary Angel Theatre Company, 105
Needles, William, 53
Nellie McClung Theatre, 107
Nelson, Harold, 29, 37, 39
Neptune Theatre, 72, 96, 112

New Brunswick Courier, 5
Newcomers, The', 82
New Dominion and True Humorist, 5
New Dominion Theatre, 10
New Empire Theatre, 29
NeWest Press, 111
Newfoundland Performing Arts Archive
    Project, 112
New Grand Theatre, 3
New Montreal Theatre, 9
New Play Centre, 85
New Play Society, 53, 68–9
New Play Society School of Drama, 74
New Venture Players, 74
New World, 100
New York Critics Drama Desk Awards,
    90
New York Idea, The, 29
New York Theatrical Syndicate, 32
New York Times, 92
Nicholas Nickleby, 79
Nickinson, John, 21, 37
Nicol, Eric, 108
Nightwood Theatre, 105, 107
90th on Active Service, The, 30
North British Review, 12
Northern Arts and Culture Centre, 112
Northern Light Theatre, 109
No Scandal in Spain, 62
Nothing to Lose, 98
Not So Dumb, 108
*Nova Scotia Chronicle and Weekly
    Advertiser*, 6
Nova Scotia Gazette, 6
*Nova Scotia Gazette and Weekly
    Chronicle*, 4
Nunn, Robert, 101, 102

O'Casey, Sean, 53, 95
O'Donoghue, W.B., 54
Oedipus, 62
Oedipus Rex, 35
Of the Fields, Lately, 89, 94
Old Vic, 55, 113
Omphale and the Hero, 75
Ondaatje, Michael, 77

One Crack Out, 95
O'Neill, James, 34
O'Neill, Nance, 38
O'Neill, Patrick, 20
One Man's House, 64
One Night Stand, 104, 107
One-person shows, 110
One Thousand Cranes, 108
One Tiger to a Hill, 101, 102
Only Way, The, 30
Ontario Arts Council, 70
On the Job, 98
On the Rim of the Curve, 97
'O.P.', 5
Open Circle, 112
Opera House (Dawson), 26
Opera House (Hanley), 27
Opera House (Vancouver), 25
Opportunities for Youth, 85
Orpheum (Dawson), 26
Orpheum (Edmonton), 29
Osborne, Colonel Henry, 57
Osborne, Marian, 48
Ostenso, Martha, 64
Othello, 39, 103
Ottawa Drama League, 49, 54
Otway, Thomas, 8
Outlook, 44
Overlaid, 54, 55
Owens, Rochelle, 85

Pacific Railway Scandal, 20
Paisley, Brian, 110
Pal Joey, 104
Palmer, John, 89
Paper Wheat, 87
Paracelsus, 82
Parker, Gilbert, 11
Pasolini/Pelosi, 105
Pasque Flower, 64
Passing of the Third Floor Back, The, 29
Patmore, Coventry, 12
Patrick, Robert, 104
Patterson, Tom, 70
Pavilion Theatre, 26
Peep O'Day, 22

Penguin Book of Modern Canadian Drama, 112
Pennington, Michael, 109
'Performance', 72
Perkyns, Richard, 112
Permanent Players, 44
Peterborough Little Theatre, 55
Peter Pan, 29
Peterson, Eric, 110
Peterson, Len, 60, 61, 72, 108
Phillips, Robin, 77, 78, 85, 100
Phoenix Theatre, 74, 112
Pier One, 85
Pierre, 48
Pierre Radisson, 48
Pinero, A.W., 35
Pinter, Harold, 91
Planchon, Roger, 86
Plant, Richard, 112
Playboy of the Western World, The, 69
Play on Words & Other Radio Plays, A, 61, 62
Playwrights Canada, 111
Plumb, Josiah Burr, 19
Plummer, Christopher, 62, 69
Poetical Tragedies, 13
Poetic drama, 12–14, 16
Point of View, The, 48
Political Intrigue, 5
Political theatre, 57–9, 81, 83, 85–6, 96, 98–9, 100, 103, 105, 107
Pollock, Sharon, 60, 77, 96, 100–2, 103, 107, 111
Ponteach, 4
Pope Joan, 107
Popular Projects Society, 59
Poutrincourt de, Jean de Biencourt, 2
Power Plays, The, 92, 93
Prague, 105, 107
Preston, Henry, 5
Price, Addison B., 7
Princess Opera House, 30, 31
Princess Theatre, 25
Prizewinner, The, 48
Professional Association of Canadian Theatres, 111

Professional organizations, 111
Progressive Arts Clubs, 58
Provincial Association, The, 5
Ptarmigan, 16, 18, 19
Publishers (drama), 111
Pygmalion, 35

Queen's Theatre, 10
'Quest', 72
Question Time, 56
Quiet in the Land, 107
Quiller, 97
Quinlan Opera Company, 29

Racine, Jean, 3
Radio drama, 12, 47, 52, 53, 59–62, 66,
   68, 97, 112
Rain, Douglas, 53, 72
Rainmaker, The, 65
Ramona and the White Slaves, 91
Rankin, McKee, 38, 39
Ray Brandon Players, 44
Real Thing, The, 109
Reaney, James, 73, 76–9, 83, 89, 92, 108
Réceptions, 3
Records of Canadian Theatre, 112
Red Emma, 88
Red Heart, The, 76
Regina Morning Leader, 28
Regina Theatre, 25, 28
Regional/civic theatres, 72, 83–5, 91,
   103, 104
Regional drama, 95–103
Reid, Kate, 46, 53, 69, 70
Reid, Leslie, 48
Reis, Kurt, 69
Renders, Kim, 107
Rex Stock Company, 44
Reynolds, Frederick, 10
Rich, Frank, 92
Richard of Bordeaux, 69
Richardson, John, 78
Richard III, 70
Richelieu, 34
Richler, Mordecai, 108
Ricketts, John B., 34

Riddle of the World, The, 95
Rideau Hall, 21
Riders to the Sea, 96
Riel, 53–4, 69
Riel, Louis, 30, 53, 54, 113
Ringwood, Gwen Pharis, 47, 60, 64–6,
   96
Risk, Sydney, 68
Rites of Passage, 107
Ritter, Erika, 88, 107
Rivals, The, 26
Roberts, Jean, 69
Robson, Frederic, 26
Rocks, 50
Rodgers, Richard, 104
Rogers, Robert, 4
'Romance of Canada, The', 60
Rosary, The, 60
Roscian Opera Company, 29
Rose, Richard, 105
Rosen, Sheldon, 77
Ross, Sinclair, 47, 64
Rossi, Ernesto, 36
Royal Alexandra Theatre, 85, 109
*Royal Gazette and Nova Scotia
   Advertiser*, 6
Royal Lyceum Theatre, 10, 37
Royal Midgets, 33
Royal Olympic Theatre, 10
Royal Ontario Museum Theatre, 69
Royal Shakespeare Company, 78, 79
Rubens, Banuta, 107
Rubes, Susan, 62
Rumours of our Death, 93
Russell, Jeanne, 29
Rutherford, John, 30
Ryan, Oscar, 58
Ryan, Toby, 57
Ryga, George, 48, 60, 65, 72, 73, 80–3,
   113

Sagouine, La, 110
Saidye Bronfman Centre, 72
St Denis, Michel, 57
Saint Joan, 38, 54
Saint John Morning News, 5

St Lawrence Centre, 56, 72, 84, 104
St. Nicholas Hotel, The, 79
SaintVallier, Bishop, 3
Sally's Choice, 53
Salt-Water Moon, 94, 95
Salutin, Rick, 87, 88
Salvini, Tommaso, 36
San Carlo Opera Company, 29
Sandwell, B.K., 43, 50
Santiago, 14
Sardou, Victorien, 39
Sarnia Little Theatre, 49
Saturday Night, 23, 50
Satyricon, The, 77
Saucy Kate, 21
Saul, 12, 13
Schellenberg, August, 81
School for Scandal, The, 3, 9
School of the National Ballet of Canada, 74
Science and Madness, 93
Scientific Socialism, 58
Scott, Duncan Campbell, 48
Scott, Munroe, 110
Scribble, Sam, 17
Seagull, The, 77, 95
Seats of the Mighty, The, 11
Second Lie, The, 48
Second Mrs Tanqueray, The, 35
Secord, Laura, 13, 48
Sentinel, The, 3
Servant of Two Masters, The, 77
Seven Oaks, 48
Seyrig, Delphine, 99
Shaffer, Peter, 84
Shakespeare Repertory Company, 38
Shakespeare, William, 7, 12, 13, 23, 29, 35, 36, 39, 75, 84, 100, 103
Shatner, William, 62
Shaw, G.B., 13, 23, 24, 35, 39, 46, 48, 49, 54, 57, 58
Shaw, Irwin, 57
Shaw Festival, 73, 104, 109, 112
Sheridan, R.B., 3, 9, 26
Shipbuilder, The, 102, 103
Shoctor Theatre, 83

Showdown at Sand Valley, 103
Shubert Theatre Corporation, 32
Silcox, J.B., 23
Simon and Pierre, 111
Simons, Beverley, 107
Simpson-Hayes, Kate, 102
Sinclair, Lister, 61-2, 69, 72
Sitting Bull, 100, 102, 113
Six Canadian Plays, 49
Six Playwrights Unit, 89
Slade, Bernard, 69
Small, Ambrose, 32, 33
Smith, Marlene, 109
Some Angry Summer Songs, 75
Sophocles, 39
Sothern E.A., 7
Splits, The, 88
Spoiled Child, The, 10
Spring Awakening, 104
Spring Gardens Theatre, 4, 7
Spring Thaw, 69
Sprung, Guy, 98, 104, 109
'Stage 44', 61
Stage in Our Past, A, 11
'Stage' radio series, 61
Stage Voices, 56
Stage West, 109
Standard Theatre, 59
Star Theatre, 22, 23
Steinbeck, John, 84
Stevens, Emily, 29
Stewart, Frances, 55
Sticks and Stones, 78
Still Stands the House, 47, 64, 113
Stock companies, 36-7, 44-5
Stonehenge Trilogy, 88
Stoppard, Tom, 65, 109
Stranger, The, 65
Stratford Festival, 7, 38, 70, 71, 73, 74, 76, 77, 78, 79, 83, 84, 86, 104, 109, 112
Stratford-on-Avon Players, 29
Stratford Shakespearean Festival (see Stratford Festival), 70
Strindberg, August, 104
Stuart, Ross, 44, 70

Studio Lab Theatre, 85
Sudbury Theatre Centre, 112
Suit of Nettles, A, 76
Sullivan, Arthur, 19, 30
Sun and the Moon, The, 76
Sunrise on Sarah, 82
Sutherland, Donald, 46
Sweet Girl Graduate, The, 13
Symphonic Expressionism, 50
Symphony, 50
Synge, J.M., 45, 47, 69, 96

Tagore, Rabindranath, 45
Tait, Michael, 11, 13
Tale of Two Cities, A, 30
Tales of Hoffman, 29
Talonbooks, 111
Tamahnous Theatre, 85, 88, 110
Tamara, 105
Taming of the Shrew, The, 29, 55
Tandy, Jessica, 77
Tannhauser, 29
Tarragon Theatre, 77, 78, 85, 88, 89,
   91, 93, 94, 95, 103, 104, 105
Tartuffe, 3, 55
Tavernier, Albert, 36, 37, 39
Tavernier Dramatic Company, 36
Tearful and Tragical Tale, The, 31
Tecumseh, 12, 13
Television drama, 53, 61, 72, 80, 82,
   93, 112
Tellegen, Lou, 29
Tempest, The, 100
Tenderfoot, The, 25
Terriss, Ellaline, 43
Terry, Ellen, 38
Terry, Harold, 44
Tey, Josephine, 69
Theatre Calgary, 72, 99, 100, 102
Theatre Canada, 52
Théâtre de la Cité, 86
*Théâtre de Neptune en la Nouvelle-
   France, Le*, 2, 3
Theatre Festival of the Americas, 110
*Theatre History in Canada, Histoire du
   théâtre au Canada*, 111

Theatre Network, 85
Theatre New Brunswick, 72, 83
Theatre of Action, 57
Theatre of the Film Noir, 93
Theatre Passe Muraille, 59, 85, 86–7,
   88, 108
Theatre Royal (Halifax), 3, 5
Theatre Royal (Montreal), 10, 16
Theatre 77, 72
Theatre 3, 85, 101, 112
Theatre 2000, 112
Theatre Workshop, 86
'Theatricus', 6
Therese's Creed, 97
They Club Seals, Don't They?, 87
Third Stage, 71, 77
This is What Happens in Orangeville,
   110
Thomas, Colin, 108
Thomas, Powys, 69
Thompson, Judith, 107
Thompson, Paul, 86–7, 110
Thompson, R.H., 109
Thorold, W.J., 37
Three Plays by George Walker, 91
Three Sisters, The, 70
Three Weddings of a Hunchback, 48
Tilley, François-Louis, 104
Tilley, Samuel, 19
Tin Flute, The, 97
Tobacco Road, 68
Toller, Ernst, 49
Toronto, 98
Toronto Arts Productions, 56
Toronto Coffee House, 9
Toronto Free Theatre, 85, 88, 91, 104
Toronto Star, 79, 89
Toronto Theatre Centre, 105
Toronto Theatre Festival, 105
Toronto Truck Theatre, 12
Toronto Workshop Productions, 59, 85,
   86
Tovell, Vincent, 54
Traill, Catherine Parr, 55
Trans-Canada Theatre Society, 32
Translation of John Snaith, The, 48

Tremayne, W.A., 14, 15
Tremblay, Michel, 89
Trespassers, 48
Trial of Louis Riel, The, 54
Triumph of Intrigue, The, 5
Turnbull, Keith, 78, 79
Twelfth Night, 29
25th Street Theatre, 85, 87, 102
Two Orphans, The, 38

Ukrainian Dramatic Ensemble, 111
Ukrainian Story Theatre for Children, 111
Uncle Tom's Cabin, 37
Uncle Vanya, 77
Unemployment, 58
Unheroic North: Four Canadian Plays, The, 46
University Magazine, 43
University of Toronto Quarterly, 54
University theatre, 63–4
Unspecific Scandal, The, 20

Van Bridge, Tony, 72
Van Cortland, Ida, 36
Vancouver Art Gallery, 81
Vancouver International Children's Festival, 108
Vancouver Little Theatre, 49
Vancouver Opera House, 27
Vancouver Playhouse, 72, 73, 80, 81, 82, 83, 101
VanderHeyden, Tina, 109
Venice Preserved, 8
Vernon, John, 69
Vertical Dreams, 88
Video Cabaret, 105
Vingoe, Mary, 107
Voaden, Herman, 49–51, 96, 112

Wacousta!, 78
Wade, Bryan, 89
Wagner, Anton, 16, 20
Waiting for the Parade, 99, 100, 103
Walker, C.P., 24, 27, 33

Walker, George, 88, 89, 91–3, 104
Walker Theatre, 25, 27, 28, 35, 59
Walsh, 100, 102
Walsh, James, 102
Warrener, Lowrie, 50
Wasserman, Jerry, 71, 112
Watt, A.B., 29, 30
Weather Breeder, The, 46, 48
Webber, Andrew Lloyd, 109
Webber, H. Price, 37
Wedekind, Frank, 104
Weiss, Peter Eliot, 110
Well of the Saints, The, 47
Wells, H.G., 58
Whisky Six, 102
White, Maureen, 107
White Biting Dog, 107
Whitney, C.J., 33
Whittaker, Herbert, 69
Widger's Way, 65
Wiebe, Rudy, 104
Wiesenfeld, Joe, 108
Wilde, Oscar, 39
Willard, E.S., 22
Williams, Tennessee, 75
Wills, Freeman, 30
Winnipeg Daily Times, 23, 30
Winnipeg Little Theatre, 72
Winnipeg Mennonite Theatre, 111
Winnipeg Theatre, 44
Wolfe, James, 48
Workers' Experimental Theatre, 57, 58

Yeats, W.B., 45, 49
Yiddish Theatre of Montreal, 111
York Colonial Advocate, 21
York Gazette, 9
You Can't Marry Your Grandmother, 3
You Can't Stop Now, 62
Young, William, 33, 39
Young People's Theatre, 108
You're a Good Man, Charlie Brown, 84
You're Gonna Be Alright, Jamie Boy, 91

Zastrozzi, 91, 92
Zoo Story, 80